Groovy Programming Language for Backend Development

Discover How Groovy Can Revolutionize Your Backend Code

Davis Simon

Discover Other Books in the Series

"Groovy Programming Language for Beginners: Your First Steps into Coding"

"Groovy Programming Language for Automation: Unlock the full potential of Groovy to streamline workflows, simplify coding"

"Groovy Programming language for Chatbots:The Ultimate Guide to Building Intelligent Chatbots with Ease"

"Groovy Programming Language for Data Science: Unlock the Power of Seamless Data Analysis and Automation"

"Groovy Programming Language for Web Development: Building Your First Web App"

"Groovy Programming Language for Big Data:Groovy to Build Scalable, Efficient, and Flexible Big Data Applications"

"Groovy Programming Language for Data Manipulation: Master the Basics and Unlock Advanced Techniques for Game-Changing Results"

"Groovy Programming Language for DevSecOps: Agile Scripting to Secure and Streamline Software Delivery With Groovy"

Disclaimer

The Book titled *"Groovy Programming Language for Backend Development: Discover How Groovy Can Revolutionize Your Backend Code"* by Davis Simon is intended for educational and informational purposes only.

The content provided in this Book is based on the author's experience, research, and personal opinions. It is designed to offer insights and techniques for backend development using the Groovy programming language.

Introduction

Welcome to **"Groovy Programming Language for Backend Development: Discover How Groovy Can Revolutionize Your Backend Code."** In an era where digital transformation is crucial, selecting the appropriate programming language can greatly influence the efficiency, scalability, and maintainability of backend systems. As organizations adapt and incorporate new technologies, developers are in search of tools that not only boost productivity but also simplify complexity. Groovy emerges as a robust, dynamic language that integrates effortlessly with the Java ecosystem while providing a more expressive and flexible syntax.

This book will delve into the distinctive features and advantages of utilizing Groovy for backend development. From its inception as a companion to Java to its rise as an independent powerhouse, Groovy has gained traction due to its simplicity and expressiveness. We will guide you through the key elements of Groovy, illustrating how it can elevate your backend projects, whether you are developing RESTful APIs, microservices, or intricate enterprise applications.

We will begin by familiarizing you with the core concepts of Groovy, emphasizing its syntax, data types, and the unique qualities that make coding both enjoyable and efficient. You will discover how to harness Groovy's dynamic features, such as closures, dynamic typing, and advanced collection manipulation, to produce clean and concise code.As we progress, we will delve into practical applications, exploring how Groovy can work alongside popular frameworks like Grails and Spring Boot, enabling you to build robust backend services that meet the demands of modern applications. You'll also discover best practices for integrating Groovy into existing Java projects and strategies for optimizing performance, ensuring that your applications are not only functional but also efficient.

Throughout this book, we will provide real-world examples, coding exercises, and tips to help you master Groovy for backend development. Our goal is to equip you with the knowledge and skills you need to revolutionize your backend code and take full advantage of what Groovy has to offer.

Whether you are a seasoned developer looking to expand your skill set or a newcomer eager to start your journey in backend programming, this book is tailored to meet your needs. Together, let's embark on a journey to discover how Groovy can transform your approach to backend development, making it smarter, faster, and more enjoyable.

Chapter 1: Introduction to Groovy for Backend Development

As the field of software development continues to progress, there has been a significant increase in the need for programming languages that are agile, efficient, and easy to maintain. One of the compelling options currently available is Groovy, a robust language that enhances Java's capabilities while offering a more dynamic and expressive syntax. This chapter aims to introduce Groovy in the realm of backend development, highlighting its features, benefits, and various applications.

1.1 What is Groovy?

Groovy is an object-oriented programming language that operates on the Java Virtual Machine (JVM). It is designed to complement Java by simplifying many of its complexities while ensuring smooth interoperability. Groovy is recognized for its succinct syntax, dynamic typing, and its ability to support domain-specific languages (DSLs). It can be utilized for a wide range of tasks, including scripting, web application development, and, notably, backend development.## 1.2 Groovy's Features ### 1.2.1 Dynamic Typing

One of Groovy's most significant features is dynamic typing. Unlike Java, where the type of a variable must be declared explicitly, Groovy allows for more flexible and concise coding practices. This results in quicker prototyping and a more straightforward coding experience. Developers can focus on logic rather than boilerplate code, leading to increased productivity.

1.2.2 Closures

Closures are another powerful feature of Groovy, enabling developers to write blocks of code that can be executed at a later time. This functional programming capability allows for more expressive and maintainable code, particularly in backend applications where data manipulation and processing are common.

1.2.3 GDK (Groovy Development Kit)

The Groovy Development Kit enhances the capabilities of the standard Java libraries, providing additional methods and utility functions that simplify common tasks. The GDK enriches the developer's toolkit, allowing for rapid application development without sacrificing performance.

1.2.4 Syntax Sugar

Groovy provides numerous syntactic conveniences that make code easier to write and read. For instance, semicolons are optional, parentheses can be omitted in certain contexts, and properties can be accessed using a more natural dot notation. This "syntax sugar" improves code clarity and reduces the learning curve for new developers.

1.3 Advantages of Using Groovy for Backend Development ### 1.3.1 Seamless Integration with Java

Being fully compatible with Java, Groovy allows developers to leverage existing Java libraries and frameworks. This means that teams can gradually introduce Groovy into their projects without the need for extensive refactoring of existing Java codebases.

1.3.2 Rapid Development

Groovy's expressive syntax and dynamic nature enable fast prototyping and development. Developers can iterate quickly, which is particularly advantageous in a backend context where requirements may evolve rapidly during the development process.

1.3.3 Support for Modern Frameworks

Frameworks such as Grails, a web application framework built on Groovy, provide additional tools and conventions that streamline backend development. Grails promotes the "convention over configuration" principle, which reduces the amount of decision-making required for setup and allows developers to focus on application logic.

1.3.4 Testing and Documentation

Groovy features a robust ecosystem for testing, with Spock being a prominent testing framework designed specifically for Groovy. Its expressive syntax makes writing tests more intuitive, thus enhancing the overall quality of backend applications through better test coverage. Additionally, Groovy's annotations support automatically documenting code, which aids in maintaining clear communication within development teams.

1.4 Practical Applications of Groovy in Backend Development

Groovy is frequently employed in various backend development tasks, ranging from building RESTful APIs to developing microservices architectures. Its adaptability is evident in scenarios such as:

Web Applications: Utilizing Grails, developers can build full-stack web applications efficiently. Its integration with front-end technologies and support for database operations make it an attractive choice for modern web development.

Automation and Scripting: Groovy excels as a scripting language, enabling developers to automate mundane tasks, manage deployments, or write data processing scripts, all while benefiting from its Java interoperability.

Microservices: Groovy's lightweight nature makes it ideal for developing microservices that need to be built and deployed rapidly within a DevOps context. Its simplicity and reduced overhead aid in creating services that are maintainable and scalable.

In this introductory chapter, we have explored Groovy as a significant player in the realm of backend development. Its dynamic capabilities, seamless Java integration, and developer-friendly features position it as an excellent choice for teams seeking to enhance their development efficiency and maintainability. As we progress through this book, we will delve deeper into Groovy's syntax, advanced features, and practical applications, empowering developers to leverage this versatile language in their backend development endeavors.

Understanding Groovy: Features and Benefits

This chapter explores the key features and benefits of Groovy, illustrating why it has become a popular choice for modern software development.

Key Features of Groovy ### 1. **Dynamic Typing**

One of Groovy's standout features is its dynamic typing, which allows developers to write code without explicitly declaring data types. This flexibility can speed up development time, as it lowers the barrier to entry for writing code. For example:

```groovy
def name = "Groovy" def number = 42
```

In this example, the data types of `name` and `number` are inferred at runtime, eliminating the need for verbose type declarations seen in Java.

2. **Closures**

Groovy treats closures as first-class citizens. A closure is a block of code that can be assigned to a variable, passed as a parameter, or returned from a function. This feature provides developers with powerful constructs for functional programming, allowing for concise and expressive code:

```groovy
def square = { x -> x * x } println square(5) // Outputs: 25
```

3. **Simplified Syntax**

Groovy simplifies Java's syntax by removing boilerplate code, making it more readable and maintainable. For instance, Groovy allows us to omit semicolons and parentheses in many cases:

```groovy
def person = new Person(name: "Alice", age: 30)
```

This approach leads to cleaner code that is easier to

13

understand at a glance. ### 4. **Native Support for Collections**

Groovy provides a native and powerful way to work with collections. With built-in methods like `collect`,

`find`, and `each`, developers can manipulate collections with ease:

```groovy
def numbers = [1, 2, 3, 4, 5]
def doubled = numbers.collect { it * 2 }


rintln doubled // Outputs: [2, 4, 6, 8, 10]
```

5. **Interoperability with Java**

Groovy is designed to integrate closely with Java, utilizing Java's libraries, frameworks, and tools. This interoperability means that developers can gradually introduce Groovy into existing Java projects, reaping the benefits of the language without complete rewrites.

6. **Metaprogramming Capabilities**

Groovy's metaprogramming capabilities allow developers to modify classes, methods, and properties at runtime. This flexibility leads to powerful and dynamic applications, where behavior can be changed based on the context:

```groovy class Person {
String name
```

```
}
// Adding    a    new    method    dynamically
Person.metaClass.greet = { -> "Hello, ${name}!" }

def alice = new Person(name: "Alice") println alice.greet()
// Outputs: Hello, Alice!
```
```

## Benefits of Using Groovy

### 1. **Increased Developer Productivity**

With its concise syntax, powerful abstractions, and dynamic capability, Groovy significantly increases developer productivity. The language's simplicity allows developers to write code faster and with fewer lines, leading to quicker iterations and less frustration.

### 2. **Enhanced Testing Frameworks**

Groovy comes with powerful testing frameworks such as Spock and Geb, making it easier to write and run tests. With its expressive DSLs, developers can write specifications and tests that are clear and easy to understand.

### 3. **Support for Domain-Specific Languages (DSLs)**

Groovy's flexible syntax allows developers to create DSLs that are tailored to specific domains, simplifying processes and making code easier to communicate. This feature is particularly valuable in areas such as configuration management, build systems, and data processing.

### 4. **Growing Community and Ecosystem**

The Groovy community is vibrant and growing.

15
```

Developers can take advantage of a wide range of libraries, frameworks (like Grails for web applications), and resources for learning and collaboration.

5. **Compatibility with Existing Java Codebases**

For organizations already utilizing Java, adopting Groovy represents a low-risk option. Groovy can interoperate with existing Java code, allowing teams to leverage prior investments while evolving their codebases incrementally.

With its dynamic typing, closures, simplified syntax, and seamless interoperability with Java, Groovy enables developers to produce high-quality, maintainable code quickly and easily. Its robust features and burgeoning ecosystem make it an attractive choice for developers looking to enhance their productivity and create innovative solutions. Whether you are maintaining legacy Java projects or embarking on new ventures, Groovy offers a pathway to enhance your coding experience and output.

The Power of Groovy for Backend Development

Among the myriad of options available, Groovy emerges as a powerful contender for backend development. This chapter delves into the features, advantages, and use cases of Groovy, highlighting its unique strengths and how it integrates with other technologies to streamline backend processes.

What is Groovy?

Groovy is an agile, dynamic language for the Java Virtual

Machine (JVM) that builds upon Java's syntax and incorporates features from languages like Python, Ruby, and Smalltalk. It is designed to enhance developer productivity by providing a concise and expressive syntax while maintaining the robustness of Java.

Groovy's interoperability with Java codebase ensures that it can easily integrate with existing Java applications, libraries, and frameworks.

Key Features of Groovy ### 1. Concise Syntax

One of the most attractive features of Groovy is its concise syntax. Groovy reduces boilerplate code significantly, allowing developers to write less code to accomplish the same tasks compared to Java. For instance, in Groovy, getters and setters are automatically generated, which streamlines the process of object manipulation.

2. Dynamic Typing

While Java is statically typed, Groovy allows for dynamic typing, enabling developers to write code more flexibly. This feature can lead to quicker prototyping and simpler testing, especially in scenarios where the exact data types might not be known at compile time.

3. Simplified Syntax for Collections

Groovy extends the Java Collections Framework with a range of syntactic shortcuts and built-in capabilities. This allows developers to manipulate collections with powerful operations, such as filtering, mapping, and grouping, making code both simpler and more readable.

4. Closures

Groovy introduces the concept of closures, which are

blocks of code that can be executed at a later time. Closures support functional programming paradigms, allowing for more expressive and reusable code. This feature is particularly useful when passing behavior as arguments to methods.

5. Native Support for Domain-Specific Languages (DSLs)

Groovy's flexibility makes it an excellent choice for building domain-specific languages. With Groovy, developers can create expressive DSLs that are tailored to their application's requirements, enabling more intuitive interaction with the code.

6. Exceptional Integration

Groovy can seamlessly integrate with existing Java frameworks and libraries. It works exceptionally well with Spring, Grails, Hibernate, and other Java-based technologies. This compatibility allows teams to leverage their existing expertise in Java while adopting Groovy's powerful features. ## Advantages of Using Groovy for Backend Development

1. Rapid Development

The combination of Groovy's concise syntax, dynamic typing, and rich libraries accelerates the development process, allowing teams to iterate quickly and deliver software faster to the market.

2. Enhanced Readability and Maintainability

Groovy's expressive syntax and use of closures contribute to code that is easier to read and maintain. This aspect is invaluable in team environments, where multiple developers may be working on the same codebase.

3. Strong Community and Ecosystem

Groovy has a vibrant community and a strong ecosystem that provides extensive documentation, libraries, and frameworks that facilitate backend development. The growth of Groovy's community has also led to numerous plugins, tools, and integrations that enhance its functionality.

4. Built-in Testing Support

Groovy includes powerful testing capabilities, allowing developers to write unit tests quickly and efficiently. Frameworks like Spock, which is built on Groovy, enable Behavior-Driven Development (BDD) and make it easy to validate logic within applications.

5. Integration with Modern Practices

Groovy readily adopts modern software development practices, including microservices architecture, continuous integration/continuous deployment (CI/CD), and cloud-native development. This adaptability ensures that teams can utilize Groovy within contemporary development paradigms.

Use Cases for Groovy in Backend Development ### 1. Web Application Development with Grails

Grails is a web application framework that uses Groovy, enabling rapid application development. By leveraging Grails' conventions and powerful features, developers can build robust web applications quickly while benefiting from Groovy's expressive code.

2. API Development

That Groovy language is an excellent choice for building

RESTful APIs due to its simplicity, performance, and the ability to work well with JSON and other data formats. Groovy's integration with Spring and other web frameworks streamlines the creation of RESTful services.

3. Scripting and Automation

Groovy is often used for scripting and automating tasks within Java applications. Its dynamic nature allows developers to execute scripts for various automation tasks, enhancing productivity and development workflow.

4. Interoperability Solutions

Applications that require integration with various systems can leverage Groovy's ability to work with different languages and technologies. Groovy scripts can act as glue code that connects disparate services, APIs, and databases.

As the demand for agile and efficient backend solutions continues to grow, embracing Groovy's potential will empower teams to meet their challenges head-on while delivering innovative products and services that stand out in today's competitive landscape. Whether through web applications, RESTful APIs, or internal automation scripts, Groovy's power in backend development is undeniable, paving the way for the next generation of software solutions.

Chapter 2: Setting Up Your Groovy Development Environment

Groovy, with its dynamic capabilities and seamless integration with Java, has gained popularity among developers for crafting applications, from simple scripts to large-scale enterprise solutions. This chapter will guide you through setting up your Groovy development environment, ensuring you have the tools and configurations necessary to optimize your coding experience.

2.1 Prerequisites

Before diving into the installation and configuration, it's crucial to check that your machine meets the following prerequisites:

2.1.1 Java Development Kit (JDK)

Groovy is built on top of Java, so a compatible Java Development Kit (JDK) must be installed. Groovy works best with JDK versions 8 or 11. You can download the JDK from the [Oracle website](https://www.oracle.com/java/technologies/javase-jdk11-downloads.html) or use an open-source variant like OpenJDK.

Installation Steps:

Download the JDK installer for your operating system.

Follow the installation instructions specific to your OS.

After installation, verify the installation by running the following command in your terminal or command prompt:

```bash
```

java -version
```

### 2.1.2 Groovy

Once you have the JDK installed, the next step is to install Groovy. The installation can be done in various ways, including using SDKMAN!, downloading a binary distribution, or using package managers available for your operating system.

#### 2.1.2.1 Using SDKMAN!

SDKMAN! is a tool for managing parallel versions of multiple Software Development Kits on most Unix- based systems. To install Groovy using SDKMAN!, follow these steps:

Open your terminal.

Install SDKMAN! by running the following command:

```bash
curl -s "https://get.sdkman.io" | bash
```

Follow the prompted instructions to complete the installation.

To install Groovy, run:

```bash
sdk install groovy

```

Verify the installation by checking the Groovy version:
```

```bash
groovy -version
```

2.1.2.2 Manual Installation

Alternatively, you can download Groovy as a ZIP file from the [Groovy website](https://groovy.apache.org/download.html) and extract it to a preferred directory. Here are the steps:

Download the latest Groovy distribution ZIP file.

Extract the ZIP file to a directory, for example, `C:\groovy` on Windows or `~/groovy` on macOS/Linux.

Add Groovy to your system's PATH environment variable:

Windows: Right-click My Computer > Properties > Advanced system settings > Environment Variables. Under System variables, find and select PATH, click Edit, and add the path to the `bin` directory (e.g., `C:\groovy\bin`).

macOS/Linux: Open a terminal and edit your shell configuration file (e.g., `~/.bashrc`,

`~/.bash_profile`, or `~/.zshrc`) and add:

```bash
export PATH=$PATH:~/groovy/bin
```

Run `source ~/.bashrc` (or the relevant file) to reload the configuration. ### 2.1.3 Integrated Development Environment (IDE)

While you can write Groovy in any text editor, utilizing an Integrated Development Environment (IDE) significantly boosts productivity. Popular IDEs for Groovy development include:

IntelliJ IDEA: A powerful IDE that supports Groovy with excellent code completion, debugging, and integration.

Eclipse with Groovy Plugin: Eclipse can be extended with Groovy plugins for a tailored development experience.

2.1.3.1 IntelliJ IDEA Setup

Download and install IntelliJ IDEA from the [JetBrains website](https://www.jetbrains.com/idea/download/).

Launch IntelliJ IDEA and create a new project.

Choose "Groovy" as the project type and specify the JDK you installed earlier.

Create a new Groovy file to start coding. #### 2.1.3.2 Eclipse Setup

Download the Eclipse IDE for Java Developers from the [Eclipse website](https://www.eclipse.org/downloads/).

Install Groovy by going to Help > Eclipse Marketplace and searching for the Groovy plugin.

Install the plugin and restart Eclipse.

Create a new Class or Groovy Script to begin development. ## 2.2 Creating Your First Groovy Script

Now that your development environment is set up, let's create a simple Groovy script to ensure everything is functioning correctly.

Open your IDE and create a new Groovy file named `HelloWorld.groovy`.

Add the following code to print "Hello, Groovy!":

```groovy
println 'Hello, Groovy!'
```

Run the script using your IDE's run command or from the terminal with:

```bash
groovy HelloWorld.groovy
```

You should see the output:

```
Hello, Groovy!
```

Setting up a Groovy development environment is a straightforward process that requires having the necessary tools like the JDK, Groovy, and a suitable IDE. Once your environment is ready, you can start leveraging Groovy's powerful features to write clean, expressive code. In the next chapter, we will delve into the fundamentals of Groovy syntax and language features, providing a solid foundation for your Groovy programming journey.

Installing Groovy and Essential Tools

This chapter will guide you through the process of installing Groovy, alongside essential tools that will enhance your backend development experience.

1. Understanding Groovy

Before diving into the installation process, it's useful to understand why Groovy is a great choice for backend development. Groovy is dynamic, has less verbose syntax compared to Java, and integrates well with existing Java codebases. This makes it highly suitable for various backend applications, from RESTful web services to complex enterprise applications.

Key Features of Groovy:

Dynamic Typing: Groovy allows for a more fluid coding experience, enabling quicker prototyping and less boilerplate code.

Closures: Groovy supports closures, which can make working with collections and functional programming constructs easier.

Compatibility: As Groovy runs on the JVM, it can leverage Java libraries and frameworks without any hassle.

Grails Framework: A powerful web application framework built on top of Groovy that accelerates development.

2. Prerequisites

Before installing Groovy, ensure that you have the

following prerequisites:

Java Development Kit (JDK): Groovy requires JDK version 8 or higher. Check if you already have it installed by running:

```bash
java -version
```

If you do not have the JDK installed, follow the steps below. ### Installing Java JDK

For Windows:

Download the JDK from [Oracle's official website](https://www.oracle.com/java/technologies/javase-jdk11-downloads.html).

Follow the installation wizard and ensure to check the box that says "Set JAVA_HOME variable."

Add `JAVA_HOME` to your system environment variables.

For macOS:

Install the JDK using Homebrew:

```bash
brew install openjdk@11
```

Set the JAVA_HOME variable in your terminal profile:

```bash
echo 'export JAVA_HOME=/usr/local/opt/openjdk@11' >> ~/.bash_profile source ~/.bash_profile
```

```

**For Linux:**

Install OpenJDK using your package manager, for example:

```bash
sudo apt install openjdk-11-jdk
```

Verify the installation with the `java -version` command.
3. Installing Groovy

With Java set up, you're ready to install Groovy. There are several methods to install Groovy, including via SDKMAN!, Homebrew, or manually installing through a ZIP file. Here, we will explore these methods.

Option 1: Using SDKMAN!

SDKMAN! is a great tool for managing parallel versions of multiple Software Development Kits, including Groovy.

Open your terminal.

Install SDKMAN! by running:

```bash
curl -s "https://get.sdkman.io" | bash
```

Follow the instructions in the terminal to complete the installation.

Reload your terminal or run:

```bash
```
```

source "$HOME/.sdkman/bin/sdkman-init.sh"
```

Install Groovy by running:
```bash
sdk install groovy
```

Option 2: Using Homebrew (macOS)

If you're on macOS and prefer using Homebrew:

Run:
```bash
brew install groovy
```

Option 3: Manually Installing Groovy

Download the latest stable release from the [Groovy website](https://groovy-lang.org/download.html).

Extract the ZIP file to a directory of your choice.

Add Groovy's `bin` directory to your PATH variable:

For Windows:

Add the path to the Groovy `bin` folder to your system variables.

For macOS/Linux:

Append the following line in your profile file (e.g., `~/.bash_profile`):
```bash

```
export PATH=$PATH:/path/to/groovy/bin
```

```

## 4. Verifying Your Installation

To confirm that Groovy is installed correctly, open a terminal and run:

```bash
groovy -version
```

You should see the version number of Groovy you just installed. This means you're all set to start coding! ## 5. Essential Tools for Back-End Development

While Groovy is powerful on its own, using accompanying tools can enhance your development process significantly. Here are some essential tools that every backend developer should consider:

Integrated Development Environment (IDE)

IntelliJ IDEA: A leading IDE for Java and Groovy development. It offers excellent support for Groovy language features and integrations.

Eclipse Groovy Plugin: If you're more comfortable with Eclipse, this plugin offers Groovy support.

Build Tool

Gradle: A build automation tool that is highly efficient when used with Groovy, allowing you to define project dependencies, build lifecycles, and more.
```

Frameworks

Grails: For developing web applications, Grails leverages Groovy to create elegant, RESTful applications rapidly. It's built on top of Spring, allowing you to use its ecosystem effortlessly.

Version Control

Git: Essential for version control, enabling you to manage code versions and collaborate with others effectively. Familiarize yourself with platforms like GitHub or GitLab for repository hosting.

With Groovy installed and the essential tools ready, you're now equipped to embark on your backend development journey. Groovy's simplicity, combined with the right frameworks and tools, empowers you to build robust and maintainable applications. In the next chapter, we'll dive into fundamental Groovy concepts and syntax to get your coding skills up to speed. Happy coding!

Creating Your First Groovy Script

Groovy leverages the robust capabilities of Java while adding features that enhance code productivity and readability.

In this chapter, we will walk through the steps of creating your first Groovy script, setting up the environment, and deploying it in a backend application. This provides a solid foundation for further exploring Groovy's capabilities in web development, API service creation, and more.

Setting Up Your Development Environment

Before diving into coding, you need to set up your development environment. Here's how to do it. ### Step 1: Install Java Development Kit (JDK)

Groovy runs on the JVM, so you need to have the JDK installed on your machine. You can download the latest version of JDK from [Oracle's official site](https://www.oracle.com/java/technologies/javase-jdk11- downloads.html) or adopt OpenJDK from [AdoptOpenJDK](https://adoptopenjdk.net/).

Step 2: Install Groovy

The easiest way to get Groovy up and running is to use SDKMAN, a tool for managing parallel versions of multiple Software Development Kits:

Open your terminal (or command prompt) and install SDKMAN:

```bash
curl -s "https://get.sdkman.io" | bash
```

After installation, restart your terminal and run:

```bash
sdk install groovy
```

You can verify the installation by running:

```bash
groovy --version
```

Step 3: Set Up Your IDE

While you can write Groovy scripts in any text editor, using an Integrated Development Environment (IDE) like IntelliJ IDEA or Eclipse enhances your productivity. Both IDEs have excellent support for Groovy.

IntelliJ IDEA: Download from [JetBrains](https://www.jetbrains.com/idea/download/).

Eclipse: If you prefer Eclipse, make sure to install the Groovy plugin from the Eclipse Marketplace. ## Writing Your First Groovy Script

Now that your environment is set up, let's create your first Groovy script. ### Step 1: Create a New File

Open your IDE and create a new file named `HelloWorld.groovy`. ### Step 2: Write Your Script

Enter the following Groovy code:

```groovy
// HelloWorld.groovy println 'Hello, World!'
```

This simple script outputs "Hello, World!" to the console. ### Step 3: Run Your Script

To run your Groovy script, you can either use your IDE's built-in capability or run it from the command line. #### Running from the IDE

Simply right-click on the `IIelloWorld.groovy` file and select "Run." #### Running from the Command Line

Open your terminal, navigate to the directory where

`HelloWorld.groovy` is located, and run:
```bash
groovy HelloWorld.groovy
```

You should see the output:
```

Hello, World!
```

Enhancing Your Script

Now that you've created a basic script, let's enhance it with some functionalities relevant to backend development.

Step 1: Create a Simple REST API

Groovy integrates seamlessly with frameworks like Grails and Spring Boot. For demonstration, we will create a simple REST API using Groovy's built-in HTTP capabilities.

First, install the necessary dependencies. If using Gradle, your `build.gradle` file should include:
```groovy
dependencies {
implementation 'org.codehaus.groovy:groovy-all:3.0.9'
implementation 'org.springframework.boot:spring-boot-starter-web:2.5.4'
}
```

Step 2: Create the REST Controller

Create a new Groovy file named `HelloController.groovy` with the following code:

```groovy
import org.springframework.boot.SpringApplication
import org.springframework.boot.autoconfigure.SpringBootApplication
import org.springframework.web.bind.annotation.GetMapping
import org.springframework.web.bind.annotation.RestController

@SpringBootApplication class Application {

static void main(String[] args) {
SpringApplication.run(Application, args)
}
}

@RestController

class HelloController { @GetMapping("/hello") String hello() {

return 'Hello, World!'
}
}
```

Step 3: Run the Application

Run your Spring Boot application from your IDE or terminal. Once the application is running, navigate to

35

`http://localhost:8080/hello` in your browser or use a tool like Postman to send a GET request. You should see:

```
Hello, World!
```

In this chapter, we covered the basics of setting up your development environment for Groovy, writing your first script, and creating a simple REST API. As you continue learning Groovy, you'll discover its rich features for backend development, integration with powerful frameworks like Spring and Grails, and how it can improve your coding efficiency.

Chapter 3: Groovy Syntax and Language Fundamentals

Groovy is an object-oriented language for the Java platform, known for its succinctness and agility in expressing ideas. By introducing dynamic typing, a cleaner syntax, and powerful built-in features, Groovy enhances Java's functionality, making it a favorite among developers for both scripting and building large- scale applications.

3.1 Introduction to Groovy

Groovy is designed to be a language that integrates seamlessly with Java, enabling developers to leverage both Groovy and Java code within the same project. This interoperability is one of Groovy's largest advantages, allowing for incremental adoption without the need to abandon existing Java projects.

3.2 Basic Syntax

3.2.1 Variable Declaration

In Groovy, variable declaration does not require specifying a type explicitly, thanks to its dynamic typing. Here are a few examples:

```groovy
def name = "Alice"  // String variable def age = 30     // Integer variable def height = 5.7        // Float variable
```

The `def` keyword is used to declare variables, but you can also use type annotations if you want to enforce a specific type, e.g., `String name`.

3.2.2 Data Types

Groovy supports all primitive and reference types available in Java, along with additional data types such as lists, maps, and ranges. Common data types include:

Strings: Enclosed in single or double quotes.

Lists: Defined with brackets, e.g., `def colors = ['Red', 'Green', 'Blue']`.

Maps: Created using key-value pairs, e.g., `def person = [name: 'Alice', age: 30]`.

Ranges: Defined using the `..` syntax, e.g., `def range = 1..10`. #### 3.2.3 Control Structures

Groovy includes standard control structures like `if`, `else`, `for`, `while`, and `switch`, yet it provides a more concise syntax. For example, here's a `for` loop:

```groovy
for (int i = 0; i < 5; i++) { println "Number: $i"
}
```

This syntax is similar to Java's but can be simplified with Groovy's support for closures. ### 3.3 Closures

One of Groovy's most powerful features is the closure, which is a block of code that can be assigned to a variable, passed as an argument, or returned as a value. Closures allow for functional programming paradigms. Here's how to define and use a closure:

```groovy
def greet = { name -> println "Hello, $name!" }
```

38

```groovy
greet("Bob")
```

In this example, `greet` is a closure that takes a parameter `name` and prints a greeting. Closures can also capture variables from their surrounding scope, which makes them ideal for callbacks and event handling.

3.4 Object-Oriented Features

Groovy is fully object-oriented and offers a simple yet powerful way to define classes:

```groovy
groovy class Person {

String name int age


void introduce() {

println "My name is $name and I'm $age years old."

}

}

def person = new Person(name: 'Alice', age: 30)
person.introduce()
```

In this code snippet, we define a `Person` class with properties and a method. We instantiate a `Person` object and call its method to display information.

3.5 String Interpolation and GString

Groovy introduces the concept of GString, which allows for string interpolation. By using the dollar sign `$`, we can embed variables or expressions directly into strings:

```groovy
def name = "Bob"
def greeting = "Hello, $name!"
println greeting // Output: Hello, Bob!
```

For more complex expressions, you can use `${}`:

```groovy
def x = 10
def result = "The value is: ${x * 2}" println result //
Output: The value is: 20
```

3.6 Exception Handling

In Groovy, exception handling follows the same principles
as Java but with a slightly cleaner syntax:

```groovy
try {
// Code that may throw an exception
} catch (Exception e) {
println "An error occurred: $e.message"
} finally {
println "Execution completed."
}
```

The `catch` block can catch specific exceptions, allowing
for fine-grained error handling. ### 3.7 Best Practices

While Groovy allows for a more flexible and less verbose coding style, adhering to best practices is crucial for maintainability:

Use meaningful variable names: This enhances code readability.

Utilize closures wisely: Closures can simplify code but overusing them can lead to obfuscation.

Keep methods short: Aim for methods that accomplish a single task.

Write tests: Groovy offers great support for testing frameworks like Spock and JUnit; leverage them to ensure code quality.

We learned about its dynamic typing, closures, object-oriented features, and other syntactic conveniences that make coding in Groovy enjoyable and efficient. Groovy's elegant syntax and powerful language features not only simplify code but also enhance productivity. In the next chapter, we will dive deeper into Groovy's advanced features, including its support for domain-specific languages (DSLs) and metaprogramming capabilities.

Key Syntax Elements for Backend Development

This chapter will explore the key syntax elements of Groovy that are particularly useful for backend development, highlighting its unique features and how they can enhance productivity and code maintainability.

1. Basic Syntax and Data Types

Groovy offers a combination of static and dynamic typing, providing developers with the flexibility to choose the most suitable approach for their application. The common data types in Groovy include:

Numbers: Integers and floating-point values can be defined without explicit type declarations.

```groovy
def age = 30  // Integer def price = 19.99        // Float
```

Strings: Strings in Groovy can be defined using single quotes (``) or double quotes (`"`). Double- quoted strings support GString, which allows for string interpolation.

```groovy
def name = 'John'

def greeting = "Hello, ${name}" // String interpolation
```

Collections: Groovy simplifies working with collections like Lists and Maps.

```groovy
def list = [1, 2, 3, 4, 5]        // List

def map = [name: 'John', age: 30] // Map
```

2. Control Structures

Groovy provides several control structures that streamline the execution of code blocks:

If-Else Statements:

```groovy
if (age >= 18) { println "Adult"
} else {
println "Minor"
}
```

Switch Statement:
```groovy switch (age) {
case 18:
println "Just became an adult" break
case 21:

println "Just became legal in the US" break
default:
println "Age is ${age}"
}
```

Loops: Groovy supports `for`, `while`, and `each` loop constructs for iterative operations.
```groovy
// Using each to iterate through a list list.each { num ->
println "Number: ${num}"
}
```

```groovy
// Using a for loop
for (int i = 0; i < 5; i++) { println "Index: ${i}"
}
```

3. Methods and Closures

Defining methods in Groovy is straightforward, allowing for concise and readable code. Moreover, Groovy's first-class closures make it adept for functional programming paradigms.

Methods:

```groovy
def add(int a, int b) { return a + b
}
println add(5, 10)  // Outputs: 15
```

Closures: A closure is a block of code that can take parameters and be passed around or assigned to variables.

```groovy
def multiply = { int x, int y -> x * y } println multiply(4, 5)
// Outputs: 20
```

4. Exception Handling

In backend development, robust error handling is crucial. Groovy employs `try-catch` blocks to manage exceptions seamlessly.

```groovy
try {
def result = 10 / 0
} catch (ArithmeticException e) {
println "Error occurred: Division by zero"
} finally {
println "Execution complete"
}
```

5. Object-Oriented Programming

Groovy is fully object-oriented and allows for classes, inheritance, and polymorphism.

Defining a Class:

```groovy
class Person {
String name int age
String introduce() {
return "Hi, I'm ${name} and I'm ${age} years old."
}
}
def john = new Person(name: 'John', age: 30) println
john.introduce()
```

Inheritance:

```groovy
```

```groovy
class Employee extends Person { String position
}
def employee = new Employee(name: 'Jane', age: 25,
position: 'Developer') println employee.introduce() //
Inherited method call
```

6. Integrating with Java

One of Groovy's most significant advantages is its
interoperability with Java. You can leverage existing Java
libraries or frameworks directly in Groovy code.

```groovy
import java.util.Date

def today = new Date()

println "Today's date: ${today}"
```

By understanding these key components, you can harness
Groovy's capabilities effectively in your backend
development projects, whether building REST APIs,
microservices, or data processing applications. As you
dive deeper into Groovy, you will discover even more
advanced features that can elevate your programming
experience and enhance the performance of your
applications.

Writing Cleaner and More Efficient Code

Groovy is a powerful, dynamic language for the Java Virtual Machine (JVM) that enhances Java's expressiveness while keeping its robustness. As organizations shift to more agile development practices, the need for writing cleaner and more efficient code becomes ever more pressing, particularly in the context of backend development. This chapter aims to provide best practices and approaches for crafting Groovy code that is not only clean and maintainable but also efficient.

1. Embrace Groovy's Syntax Features

Groovy's syntax offers many shortcuts which can significantly clean up your code: #### 1.1. Simplification with Type Inference

In Groovy, variables are dynamically typed, which reduces boilerplate code:

```groovy
def users = ['Alice', 'Bob', 'Charlie']
```

Using `def` allows you to avoid declaring types explicitly, whereas in Java, you'd have to declare

`List<String> users`. #### 1.2. Use of GStrings

GStrings (Groovy Strings) allow for simpler string interpolation:

```groovy
def name = "Alice" println "Hello, $name!"
```

This concatenation is cleaner and easier to read than the

equivalent in Java. ### 2. Leverage Groovy Collections and Functional Programming

Groovy provides enhanced collection manipulation capabilities that can lead to cleaner code. #### 2.1. Collection Methods

Using methods like `each`, `find`, `collect`, and `filter` can help eliminate verbose loops:

```groovy
def evenNumbers = (1..10).findAll { it % 2 == 0 }
```

This concise functional style is more readable than a traditional for-loop. #### 2.2. Using Closures for Logic Encapsulation

Closures are a powerful feature in Groovy that allows for encapsulating logic in a reusable fashion:

```groovy
def printWithPrefix = { prefix, name -> println "$prefix $name" }

['Alice', 'Bob', 'Charlie'].each { printWithPrefix("Hello", it)
}
```

This example showcases how closures can simplify operations that might otherwise require more boilerplate code.

3. Adopt Convention Over Configuration

Groovy's convention-over-configuration philosophy can help you reduce overhead and unnecessary complexity in your code.

3.1. Use Frameworks That Align with Groovy's Philosophy

Utilize frameworks such as Grails or Spring Boot that allow for minimal configuration, better file conventions, and well-defined structures. Following recommended structures helps promote clean and efficient code.

4. Optimize Performance

While Groovy's dynamic nature allows for rapid development, it can sometimes lead to performance hits. Optimize your code where possible.

4.1. Favor Static Compilation When Appropriate

Groovy supports static compilation, offering performance improvements without sacrificing code readability:

```groovy
@CompileStatic

def add(int a, int b) { return a + b

}
```

Using `@CompileStatic` enables the Groovy compiler to perform type checks and optimizations at compile time, leading to more efficient bytecode output.

4.2. Avoid Unnecessary Object Creation

Minimize object creation in performance-critical areas. Use primitive types when possible and leverage Groovy's metadata instead of creating new instances:

```groovy
def list = [1, 2, 3, 4] // Better for performance than
creating wrapper classes repeatedly.
```

5. Implement Error Handling Effectively

Clean and efficient code is also resilient. Properly handling exceptions will lead to fewer runtime errors and cleaner logic.

5.1. Use Try-Catch Wisely

Wrap only sections of code that may throw exceptions, and provide meaningful messages in catch blocks:

```groovy
try {
// potential issue area
} catch (SpecificException e) { log.error("Error occurred: ${e.message}")
}
```

5.2. Leverage Groovy's Built-in Exception Classes

Use Groovy-specific exceptions where appropriate, such as `GroovyRuntimeException`, to keep your error handling concise and accurate.

6. Write Tests First—TDD Approach

Using a Test-Driven Development (TDD) approach encourages writing cleaner code by forcing you to think about the interface and expected behavior before actual implementation.

6.1. Spock Framework

The Spock framework is a popular choice in the Groovy ecosystem, offering a powerful testing DSL:

```groovy
import spock.lang.Specification

class UserServiceSpec extends Specification { def "should create a user"() {

setup: "initialize service"

def service = new UserService()

when: "creating a user"

User user = service.createUser("Alice")

then: "the user should be created successfully" user.name == "Alice"

}

}
```

This clarity not only improves code quality but also enhances maintenance and onboarding for new developers.

By organizing your code thoughtfully, utilizing Groovy's capabilities such as closures and collections, implementing solid error handling, and committing to testing, you will significantly enhance both the quality of your code and the maintainability of your applications. As you continue to evolve your Groovy skills, remember that the principles of clean coding and efficiency are grounded in clarity, simplicity, and shared understanding among the development team.

Chapter 4: Object-Oriented Programming in Groovy

Object-Oriented Programming (OOP) is a paradigm designed to structure software in a way that captures the complexity of the real world through objects. OOP is centered around the concepts of classes and objects, encapsulation, inheritance, and polymorphism. Groovy, a powerful dynamic language for the Java platform, embraces OOP principles while providing features that enhance productivity and simplicity.

In this chapter, we will explore the fundamental aspects of OOP in Groovy, showcasing how Groovy simplifies the development process while adhering to OOP concepts. We will examine how to define classes, create objects, utilize inheritance, implement polymorphism, and create a flexible design using interfaces and abstract classes.

1. Classes and Objects

In Groovy, a class is defined using the `class` keyword, and the instantiation of a class creates an object. A class can contain fields (attributes) and methods (functions) which define the behavior of the created objects.

1.1 Defining a Class

Let's start by defining a simple `Person` class:

```groovy
class Person {

String name int age

// Constructor

Person(String name, int age) { this.name = name

this.age = age
```

53

```
}
// Method
String introduce() {
return "Hello, my name is ${name} and I am ${age} years
old."
}
}
```

In this example:

`name` and `age` are fields.

The constructor initializes the fields when a new `Person`
object is created.

The `introduce()` method returns a string that includes
the person's details. ### 1.2 Creating Objects

You can create an instance of the `Person` class as
follows:

```groovy
def person1 = new Person("Alice", 30)
println(person1.introduce())  // Output: Hello, my name
is Alice and I am 30 years old.
```

2. Encapsulation

Encapsulation is an OOP principle that restricts access to
certain components of an object. Groovy supports this

through the use of access modifiers.

2.1 Access Modifiers

In Groovy, fields can be defined as `public`, `private`, or `protected`. By default, all members are `public`.

```groovy
class BankAccount { private double balance

BankAccount(double initialBalance) { this.balance = initialBalance
}

double getBalance() { return balance
}

void deposit(double amount) { balance += amount
}

void withdraw(double amount) { if (amount <= balance) {

balance -= amount
} else {

println("Insufficient funds")
}
}
}
```

In this `BankAccount` class:

The `balance` field is private, preventing direct access from outside the class.

Public methods `getBalance()`, `deposit()`, and `withdraw()` provide controlled access to the field. ## 3. Inheritance

Inheritance allows a new class to inherit properties and methods from an existing class, promoting code reuse and logical organization.

3.1 Creating a Subclass

Here's how to create a subclass of the `Person` class, called `Employee`:

```groovy
class Employee extends Person {


String position
Employee(String name, int age, String position) {
super(name, age) // Call to the superclass constructor
this.position = position
}
@Override
String introduce() {
return super.introduce() + " I work as a ${position}."
}
}
```

In this example:

The `Employee` class inherits from the `Person` class.

The `introduce()` method is overridden to include the employee's position. ### 3.2 Using the Subclass

To create an `Employee` object, you can do:

```groovy
def employee1 = new Employee("Bob", 25, "Software Developer")

println(employee1.introduce()) // Output: Hello, my name is Bob and I am 25 years old. I work as a Software Developer.
```

4. Polymorphism

Polymorphism enables you to use a single interface or method name to refer to different underlying forms (data types). Method overriding and interface implementation are common ways to achieve polymorphism in Groovy.

4.1 Method Overriding

As seen in the `Employee` class, method overriding allows a subclass to provide a specific implementation of a method that is already defined in its superclass.

4.2 Interfaces

Interfaces define a contract that implementing classes must follow. Here's an example:

```groovy
interface Payable {

void makePayment(double amount)

}
```

```
class FreelanceWorker implements Payable { String name
FreelanceWorker(String name) { this.name = name
}
@Override
void makePayment(double amount) {
println("${name} received a payment of \$${amount}.")
}
}
```

The `FreelanceWorker` class implements the `Payable` interface. To use polymorphism, create a list of
`Payable` objects:

```groovy
def workers = [new Employee("Alice", 30, "Designer"),
new FreelanceWorker("Charlie")]
workers.each { worker ->
if (worker instanceof Payable) {
worker.makePayment(1000.0) // This will call the correct method based on the object type
}
}
```

5. Abstract Classes
An abstract class is a class that cannot be instantiated and

is meant to be subclassed. It can contain abstract methods (without implementation) that subclasses must implement.

5.1 Defining an Abstract Class

```groovy
abstract class Shape { abstract double area()

}
```

5.2 Creating Subclasses of Abstract Classes

```groovy
class Circle extends Shape { double radius

Circle(double radius) { this.radius = radius

}

@Override double area() {

return Math.PI * radius * radius

}

}

class Rectangle extends Shape { double length

double width

Rectangle(double length, double width) { this.length = length

this.width = width

}

@Override double area() {
```

```
return length * width
}
}
```
```

You can instantiate the subclasses and invoke the `area()` method polymorphically:

```groovy
def shapes = [new Circle(5), new Rectangle(4, 5)]
shapes.each { shape ->
println("Area: ${shape.area()}")
}
```

In this chapter, we have covered the fundamentals of defining classes and objects, encapsulation, inheritance, polymorphism, and abstract classes. These principles empower developers to create modular, maintainable, and scalable applications. As you continue working with Groovy, leveraging OOP will enhance your ability to handle complex systems efficiently and effectively.

Classes, Objects, and Methods

Groovy, a versatile and dynamic language for the Java platform, embraces these object-oriented principles while also providing a more concise and expressive syntax. This chapter delves into the fundamental concepts of classes, objects, and methods in Groovy, illustrating how they
```

enable developers to write cleaner, more maintainable code.

1. Understanding Classes in Groovy

A class in Groovy serves as a blueprint for creating objects. It defines properties (attributes or fields) and methods (functions or behaviors) that the objects created from the class will possess. Groovy classes are easy to define and can employ modifications such as constructors, inheritance, and interfaces.

1.1 Defining a Class

To define a class in Groovy, the `class` keyword is used, followed by the class name. A typical class definition includes fields and methods. Below is an example:

```groovy
class Person {

String name int age

// Constructor

Person(String name, int age) { this.name = name

this.age = age

}

// Method to return a description String describe() {

return "$name is $age years old."

}

}
```

In this example, the `Person` class has two properties: `name` (of type `String`) and `age` (of type `int`). A constructor initializes these fields when creating an instance of the class, and the `describe` method returns a string representing the person.

1.2 Inheritance

One of the powerful features of classes in Groovy is inheritance, allowing one class to inherit properties and methods from another. This promotes code reuse and establishes a relationship between classes. For instance:

```groovy
class Student extends Person { String studentId

Student(String name, int age, String studentId) {
super(name, age)

this.studentId = studentId

}


String describe() {

return "${super.describe()} Student ID: $studentId"

}
}
```

Here, the `Student` class inherits from the `Person` class and adds a new property, `studentId`. The `super` keyword calls the constructor of the parent class.

2. Creating and Using Objects

Once a class is defined, we can create objects (or instances) that represent specific entities based on the

62

class. In Groovy, creating an object is straightforward:

```groovy
def person = new Person("Alice", 30)

println person.describe() // Outputs: Alice is 30 years old.

def student = new Student("Bob", 22, "S123456")

println student.describe() // Outputs: Bob is 22 years old. Student ID: S123456
```

In the above example, we created `person` and `student` objects from the `Person` and `Student` classes, respectively, and called their `describe` methods to print their information.

3. Defining Methods

Methods in Groovy allow the encapsulation of behavior. They can perform actions, return data, and manipulate object state. A method is defined by specifying the return type (or using `void` for no return), followed by the method name, parameters, and body.

3.1 Method Overloading

Groovy supports method overloading, which means you can define multiple methods in a class with the same name but different parameter lists:

```groovy
class Calculator {

int add(int a, int b) { return a + b

}
```

```
double add(double a, double b) { return a + b
}
int add(int a, int b, int c) { return a + b + c
}
}
```

In this `Calculator` class, the `add` method is overloaded to handle both integer and double parameters, as well as a version that takes three integers.

3.2 Default Parameters

Groovy also supports default parameters, making method calls simpler and more flexible:

```groovy
class Greeter {
String greet(String name = "World") { return "Hello, $name!"
}
}
```

This method can be called with or without an argument:

```groovy
def greeter = new Greeter()
println greeter.greet()       // Outputs: Hello, World!
println greeter.greet("Alice") // Outputs: Hello, Alice!
```

Groovy's simplified syntax and powerful features, such as inheritance and method overloading, enable the creation of robust and maintainable code. Understanding these concepts lays the foundation for effective programming in Groovy and opens the door to advanced topics in the language and its ecosystem.

Leveraging Inheritance, Polymorphism, and Interfaces

Among its robust features, object-oriented programming (OOP) principles stand as the cornerstone that enables developers to design extensible, reusable, and maintainable applications. This chapter delves into Groovy's implementation of inheritance, polymorphism, and interfaces, emphasizing how these concepts enhance code quality and flexibility.

1. Understanding Inheritance in Groovy ### 1.1 What is Inheritance?

Inheritance allows a class to inherit properties and behavior (methods) from another class. This mechanism promotes code reusability and establishes a natural hierarchy between classes, often referred to as a parent-child relationship.

1.2 Implementing Inheritance in Groovy

In Groovy, inheritance can be defined using the `extends` keyword. The child class (subclass) inherits the properties and methods of the parent class (superclass). Here's a simple example:

```groovy
class Animal {
String name
void speak() {
println "$name makes a sound."
}
}

class Dog extends Animal { void speak() {
println "$name barks."
}
}

def dog = new Dog(name: 'Buddy') dog.speak() // Output:
Buddy barks.
```

In this example, the `Dog` class extends the `Animal` class. It overrides the `speak` method to provide its specific implementation. The ability to override methods promotes customization of inherited behavior.

1.3 Benefits of Inheritance

Code Reusability: Share common functionality among multiple classes.

Organization: Helps organize code in a hierarchical structure, making it easier to manage and understand.

Polymorphism: Enables dynamic method resolution based on the object's type at runtime.

2. Exploring Polymorphism ### 2.1 What is Polymorphism?

Polymorphism refers to the ability of different classes to be treated as instances of the same class through a common interface or superclass. In Groovy, polymorphism is primarily achieved through method overriding and dynamic method dispatch.

2.2 Method Overriding in Groovy

Polymorphism manifests itself in Groovy via method overriding. As demonstrated in the previous example, the `speak` method is overridden in the `Dog` class. We can further explore polymorphism:

```groovy
class Cat extends Animal { void speak() {

println "$name meows."

}
}

def animals = [new Dog(name: 'Buddy'), new Cat(name: 'Whiskers')] animals.each { it.speak() }
// Output:
// Buddy barks.
// Whiskers meows.

```

In this example, both `Dog` and `Cat` are treated as `Animal` objects. The `speak` method is polymorphic; it calls the overridden method based on the instance type, allowing for cleaner and more flexible code.

2.3 Advantages of Polymorphism

Flexibility and Extensibility: Easily add new classes without modifying existing code.

Interface Implementation: Achieves method signatures that can be utilized interchangeably across different classes.

3. Interfaces in Groovy ### 3.1 What is an Interface?

An interface in Groovy defines a contract for classes that implement it. Interfaces cannot contain concrete methods (though Groovy allows default methods), only method signatures and properties.

3.2 Defining and Implementing Interfaces

Using interfaces involves the `implements` keyword. Here's an example of defining an interface and implementing it in classes:

```groovy
interface Musical { void play()
}
class Piano implements Musical { void play() {


println "Playing the piano."
}
}
class Guitar implements Musical { void play() {
println "Strumming the guitar."
}
```

```
}
def instruments = [new Piano(), new Guitar()]
instruments.each { it.play() }
// Output:
// Playing the piano.
// Strumming the guitar.
```

In this case, both `Piano` and `Guitar` implement the `Musical` interface, allowing them to be treated interchangeably in collections that require a `Musical` type.

3.3 Benefits of Using Interfaces

Decoupling: Classes can operate independently of implementation details.

Multiple Inheritance: Classes can implement multiple interfaces, allowing for more flexible designs.

Contract Enforcement: Ensures that classes conform to specified behaviors.

By understanding and applying these fundamental OOP principles, Groovy developers can craft elegant solutions that adhere to software design best practices. As we continue to explore advanced Groovy features and patterns, these foundational concepts will be pivotal in building sophisticated applications that are both reliable and intuitive.

Chapter 5: Working with Ratpack Framework

In the realm of modern web application development, the choice of framework can significantly impact the efficiency and quality of the application. Ratpack, a set of Groovy-based libraries for building web applications, stands out for its simplicity, performance, and asynchronous capabilities. This chapter dives deep into the Ratpack framework, guiding you through its features, architecture, and practical implementation.

5.1 What is Ratpack?

Ratpack is a framework that facilitates the creation of asynchronous web applications using Groovy (and Java). Inspired by frameworks like Express.js in the Node.js ecosystem, Ratpack focuses on providing a high-throughput, low-latency environment for building APIs and microservices. By leveraging Groovy's dynamic nature, Ratpack minimizes boilerplate code, allowing developers to focus on writing clean and efficient business logic.

Key Features of Ratpack

Asynchronous Processing: Ratpack's non-blocking architecture means that it can handle multiple requests concurrently, making it ideal for applications that require high scalability.

Minimalistic and Modular: With a focus on composition, Ratpack applications are usually built from small, composable components rather than being monolithic.

Flexible Routing: Ratpack provides intuitive routing mechanisms that allow for easy management of various endpoints within an application.

Built-in Support for Testing: Ratpack comes equipped with testing modules that help developers write comprehensive unit and integration tests.

5.2 Setting Up Ratpack

To get started with Ratpack, you need to set up your development environment. Follow these steps to create a simple Ratpack application.

Prerequisites

Java Development Kit (JDK) 8 or higher

Apache Maven or Gradle (for project management) ### Creating a New Project

Here is how to create a new Ratpack project using Gradle.

Create a new directory for your project:

```bash
mkdir ratpack-demo cd ratpack-demo
```

Initialize a Gradle project:

```bash gradle init
```

Add the Ratpack dependency: Open the `build.gradle` file and add Ratpack dependencies to it:

```groovy plugins {
```

```
id 'groovy' id 'java'
}
repositories { mavenCentral()
}
dependencies {
implementation      'io.ratpack.ratpack-groovy:ratpack-
groovy:1.8.0'     implementation     'io.ratpack.ratpack-
core:ratpack-core:1.8.0'
}
```
`` `

Create the main application file: In the `src/main/groovy` directory, create a file named

`App.groovy`.

```groovy
import ratpack.groovy.Groovy.ratpack
ratpack { handlers {
get("hello") {
render "Hello, Ratpack!"
}
}
}
```

Run the application: You can start your Ratpack application by running the following command:

```bash
gradle run
```

Open your browser and navigate to `http://localhost:5050/hello` to see the output. ## 5.3 Understanding Ratpack Architecture

Key Components

Handlers: Handlers are the core building blocks in Ratpack. Every HTTP request is processed by a chain of handlers, making it easy to separate logic and manage routing.

Context: The Ratpack context provides a scope for managing request and response data, as well as lifecycle management.

Providers: Ratpack allows you to define providers that can be used to interpolate components into your application. They are useful for dependency injection and resource management.

5.4 Building a REST API with Ratpack ### Adding Routes

Let's enhance our Ratpack application to handle multiple RESTful endpoints. Update the `App.groovy` file to include CRUD operations for a simple in-memory user management system.

```groovy
import ratpack.groovy.Groovy.ratpack import ratpack.exec.Promise

class User { String id String name
```

73

```
User(String id, String name) { this.id = id
this.name = name
}
}
def users = [:] // In-memory store ratpack {
handlers { get("users") {
render users.values() // Return all users
}
post("users") { request -> request.body.text.then { name -
>
def id = UUID.randomUUID().toString() def user = new
User(id, name)
users[id] = user
response.status(201).send("User created with ID: ${id}")
}
}
get("users/:id") { String id -> def user = users[id]
if (user) { render user
} else {
response.status(404).send("User not found")
}
}

delete("users/:id") { String id -> if(users.remove(id)) {
```

```
response.status(204).send() // No content
} else {

response.status(404).send("User not found")
}
}
}
}
```

Testing the API

You can test your API using tools like Postman or curl. Here are some examples:

- **Create a User**:

```bash
curl -X POST http://localhost:5050/users -d "John Doe"
```

- **Get All Users**:

```bash
curl http://localhost:5050/users
```

- **Get User by ID**:

```bash
curl http://localhost:5050/users/{id}
```

```
```

- **Delete User by ID**:

```bash
curl -X DELETE http://localhost:5050/users/{id}
```

5.5 Error Handling

Handling errors gracefully is crucial for any web application. Ratpack allows you to set up global error handling that can intercept and manage exceptions. Here's an example to catch exceptions globally:

```groovy
ratpack {

handlers { all {

try {

next()

} catch (Exception e) {

response.status(500).send("Internal Server Error: ${e.message}")

}

}

// Define your routes here...

}

}

```

In this chapter, we've explored the Ratpack framework, focusing on its asynchronous nature, modularity, and ease of use with Groovy. By creating a RESTful API, we learned how to set up routes, handle HTTP methods, and manage errors effectively. With its minimalistic design and powerful features, Ratpack provides a compelling option for building high-performance web applications and microservices in Groovy.

Introduction to Ratpack and Its Core Features

Among the myriad frameworks and tools used by developers, Ratpack stands out as a lightweight, reactive web application framework built in Groovy. This chapter aims to introduce Ratpack, highlighting its core features and explaining why it has garnered attention in the world of modern application development.

What is Ratpack?

Ratpack is an open-source framework designed for Java and Groovy-based web applications. It is built on top of Netty, a high-performance asynchronous event-driven network application framework, which allows Ratpack to handle a large number of connections efficiently. Its design emphasizes a functional programming style, making it intuitive for developers familiar with Groovy's expressive syntax.

While Ratpack is primarily a web framework, its capabilities extend beyond traditional web applications. It is also suitable for building RESTful APIs, microservices, and server-rendered web applications. With Ratpack, developers can create performant and maintainable applications with less boilerplate code, leading to a more enjoyable development experience.

Key Features of Ratpack

1. **Reactive Programming Model**

At the heart of Ratpack is its reactive programming model, which enables non-blocking, asynchronous processing of requests. This means that instead of waiting for each request to be processed one by one, Ratpack can handle multiple requests simultaneously, resulting in improved performance and throughput. This model is particularly advantageous in scenarios where the application is I/O-bound, such as interacting with databases or calling external APIs.

2. **Groovy Integration**

Ratpack is inherently designed to work seamlessly with Groovy, which contributes to its expressiveness and flexibility. Groovy's dynamic nature allows developers to write less code while still maintaining clarity and readability. Features like closures and concise syntax enable rapid development, making it easy to prototype and iterate on applications. Moreover, Ratpack supports both declarative and imperative programming styles, offering developers the freedom to choose their preferred approach.

3. **Built-in Dependency Injection**

Dependency injection (DI) is a design pattern used to reduce tight coupling between components in an application. Ratpack comes with built-in support for DI through the Guice framework, allowing developers to easily manage dependencies within their applications. This feature facilitates more modular code, enabling easier testing and maintenance. By defining services as dependencies, developers can enhance the scalability of their applications as they grow in complexity.

4. **Configuration and Templating**

Ratpack provides a simple and flexible configuration system that allows for easily manageable application settings. Configuration can be done via Groovy scripts or YAML files, enabling developers to define settings in a human-readable format. Additionally, Ratpack has excellent support for templating engines such as JSX and Groovy's own MarkupTemplate, making it straightforward to render HTML views and build dynamic web applications.

5. **Testing Support**

Testing is a crucial aspect of software development, and Ratpack offers several features to facilitate the testing of web applications. It provides features such as mock servers and request handlers, which simplify the process of writing unit and integration tests. Given its emphasis on a reactive model, Ratpack's testing capabilities are designed to ensure that asynchronous code is reliable and behaves as expected.

6. **Modular Architecture**

Ratpack encourages modular design through its concept of "modules." These are reusable components that encapsulate specific functionality, making it easier to integrate libraries or additional features into applications.

The modular architecture promotes the DRY (Don't Repeat Yourself) principle, allowing developers to avoid redundancy and foster code reusability.

7. **High Performance and Scalability**

One of Ratpack's standout features is its performance capabilities. Due to its non-blocking architecture, Ratpack can handle high levels of concurrency with fewer resources compared to traditional frameworks. This efficiency is critical for modern applications, which often face varying loads and demand resilience under pressure. The framework's reliance on Netty ensures that it can scale gracefully as application demands increase.

Its core features, such as a reactive programming model, seamless Groovy integration, built-in dependency injection, flexible configuration, robust testing support, modular architecture, and high scalability make it an excellent choice for developers looking to build modern web applications. As we delve deeper into this book, we will explore each of these features in detail, offering guidance and practical examples to help you harness the full potential of Ratpack for your development needs.

Building APIs with Ratpack

Ratpack, a set of Java libraries designed for developing web applications, offers a flexible and powerful platform for building APIs. Leveraging Groovy—an expressive language that compiles to Java—simplifies the process while enhancing productivity. This chapter will guide you through the essentials of building APIs with Ratpack in Groovy, focusing on the core concepts, best practices, and practical examples.

What is Ratpack?

Ratpack is a non-blocking web application framework for Java that emphasizes simplicity and performance. Designed for building microservices and RESTful APIs, Ratpack allows developers to create scalable applications without the overhead typically associated with traditional frameworks. Its modular architecture, event-driven model, and support for asynchronous programming make it an excellent choice for modern web applications.

Using Groovy with Ratpack enhances the experience. Groovy's syntax is more concise than Java, which speeds up development time and makes code easier to read and maintain. Let's delve into how to set up a Ratpack project and create a basic API.

Setting Up Your Ratpack Project

To start building an API with Ratpack in Groovy, you'll need to set up a new project. Follow these steps: ### 1. Prerequisites

Ensure you have the following installed on your machine:

Java Development Kit (JDK) 8 or later

Gradle (for managing dependencies and building your project)

Groovy (optional for inline Groovy sources, but recommended) ### 2. Create a New Gradle Project

Create a new directory for your project:

```bash
```

mkdir ratpack-api cd ratpack-api

```
```

Generate a new Gradle build file:

```bash
touch build.gradle
```

3. Configure Your `build.gradle`

Open your `build.gradle` and define the dependencies and plugins required for Ratpack:

```groovy
plugins {
id 'groovy'

id 'com.github.johnrengelman.shadow' version '7.0.0' // For creating fat JARs
}
repositories { mavenCentral()
}
dependencies {

implementation 'io.ratpack.ratpack-groovy:ratpack-groovy:1.9.0' implementation 'org.codehaus.groovy:groovy' testImplementation 'io.ratpack.ratpack-test:ratpack-test:1.9.0'

}
```

4. Create Your Main Application Class Create a new directory called `src/main/groovy`:

82

```bash
mkdir -p src/main/groovy
```

Inside this directory, create a new file named `ApiApplication.groovy` with the following content:

```groovy
import ratpack.groovy.Groovy.ratpack
ratpack { handlers {
get("api/hello") {
render "Hello, World!"
}
get("api/greet/:name") {
String name = pathTokens.name render "Hello, ${name}!"
}
}
}
```

5. Running Your Application

To run your Ratpack application, navigate back to the root directory and execute:

```bash
./gradlew run
```

You should see output indicating that Ratpack has started.

You can test the API by navigating to the following URLs in your web browser or using tools like `curl` or Postman:

`http://localhost:5050/api/hello`

`http://localhost:5050/api/greet/YourName`

Building More Complex APIs ### Request Handling

Ratpack provides a simple yet powerful abstraction for handling HTTP requests. In real-world applications, you'll often need to process incoming data, validate it, and respond accordingly. Here's an example of handling a POST request with JSON data.

First, include the JSON handling dependency in your `build.gradle`:

```groovy
implementation                'io.ratpack.ratpack-json:ratpack-json:1.9.0'
```

Then, modify your `ApiApplication.groovy`:

```groovy
import ratpack.jackson.Jackson

ratpack { handlers {

post("api/user") { request.body()

.then { body ->

def userData = Jackson.jsonParser().parse(body)

String name = userData.name render "User ${name} created!"
```

84

```
}
}
}
}
```
` ` `

Error Handling

Proper error handling is critical for maintaining the integrity of your API. Ratpack allows you to handle exceptions globally:

` ` `groovy ratpack {

error { Throwable throwable ->

response.status(500).send("Internal   Server   Error: ${throwable.message}")

}

handlers {

// your handlers here

}

}

` ` `

Middleware and Interceptors

Ratpack supports middleware, allowing you to add functionalities that apply to all requests. Here's howyou might implement logging middleware:

` ` `groovy

```groovy
import ratpack.exec.Blocking import org.slf4j.Logger
import org.slf4j.LoggerFactory

Logger logger = LoggerFactory.getLogger("API Logger")
ratpack {

before {

logger.info("Received request to ${request.getUri()}")

}

handlers {

// your handlers here

}

}
```
```

## Testing Your API

Testing is an essential aspect of API development. Ratpack provides built-in testing utilities to facilitate writing unit tests for your API. You can create a test instance of your application and verify the expected behavior:

```groovy
import io.ratpack.test.embed.EmbeddedApp import ratpack.test.UnitTest

class ApiApplicationTest extends UnitTest { void "test hello endpoint"() {

EmbeddedApp.fromInstance(ratpack {

handlers {
```
```

```
get("api/hello") { render "Hello, World!" }
}
}).test { http ->
http.get("api/hello") { response ->
assert response.body.text == "Hello, World!" assert
response.status.code == 200
}
}
}
}
```
` ` `

By leveraging the flexibility of Ratpack and the expressiveness of Groovy, you can create powerful and maintainable APIs. We covered setting up a project, handling requests, managing errors, implementing middleware, and writing tests. With these foundational skills, you're well-equipped to build your own APIs using Ratpack. As you continue to explore Ratpack, consider integrating additional features like authentication, data storage, and more advanced routing techniques to enhance your APIs further. Happy coding!

Chapter 6: Exploring Micronaut for Microservices

Among the various frameworks available for developing microservices, Micronaut stands out due to its innovative design and support for multiple JVM languages, including Groovy. In this chapter, we will delve into Micronaut and explore its benefits, features, and how to effectively create microservices using Groovy.

6.1 Introduction to Micronaut

Micronaut is a modern JVM framework designed for building microservices and serverless applications. It is lightweight, efficient, and provides several advantages over traditional frameworks, particularly when it comes to startup time and memory consumption. The key selling points of Micronaut include:

Compile-time Dependency Injection: Unlike other frameworks that rely heavily on runtime reflection, Micronaut performs dependency injection at compile time. This leads to reduced memory footprint and significantly faster startup times, making it ideal for microservices running in cloud environments.

Reactive Programming Support: Micronaut seamlessly integrates with reactive programming paradigms, allowing developers to build non-blocking applications. This is particularly useful for applications that require high concurrency and performance.

Built-in Cloud Support: Native support for various cloud platforms and features such as service discovery, configuration management, and circuit breakers make deploying Micronaut applications in the cloud a breeze.

Language Agnosticism: Although Micronaut is primarily designed for Java developers, it supports other JVM languages like Kotlin and Groovy. This allows Groovy developers to leverage the power of Micronaut while adhering to their preferred language paradigm.

6.2 Setting Up the Environment

Before we dive into coding, we need to set up our development environment to work with Micronaut and Groovy. Here's how to get started:

Install Java Development Kit (JDK): Micronaut requires JDK 8 or higher. Ensure that you have the JDK installed and configured correctly in your system.

Install Micronaut CLI: The Micronaut Command Line Interface (CLI) makes it easy to create and manage Micronaut applications. You can install it via SDKMAN! or directly from the Micronaut website.

```bash
sdk install micronaut
```

Install Groovy: Although Micronaut can be used without Groovy, we are specifically exploring the integration of Groovy in this chapter. You can install Groovy via SDKMAN! or download it from the official Groovy website.

Set up Your IDE: Popular IDEs like IntelliJ IDEA and Eclipse support Micronaut and Groovy seamlessly. Make sure to install the necessary plugins for Groovy support to take advantage of code completion and other IDE features.

89

6.3 Creating Your First Micronaut Microservice Using Groovy

Once the environment is ready, let's create a simple microservice using Micronaut and Groovy. We will build a simple REST API that manages a collection of books.

Step 1: Generate the Micronaut Application

Using the Micronaut CLI, we can generate a new project by running:

```bash
mn create-app example.micronaut.books --lang groovy
```

This command creates a new directory named `books` with a basic Micronaut project structure. ### Step 2: Creating the Model

Inside the `src/main/groovy/example/micronaut/books` directory, create a new file named `Book.groovy`. This class will represent our book model.

```groovy
package example.micronaut.books

class Book { String id String title String author

}
```

Step 3: Writing the Controller

Next, we need a controller to handle HTTP requests. Create a new file named `BookController.groovy` in the same directory.

90

```groovy
package example.micronaut.books

import io.micronaut.http.annotation.Controller  import
io.micronaut.http.annotation.Get               import
io.micronaut.http.annotation.Post              import
io.micronaut.http.annotation.Body

@Controller("/books") class BookController {

private List<Book> bookList = [] @Get("/")

List<Book> list() {

return bookList

}

@Post("/")

Book save(@Body Book book) { bookList.add(book)

return book

}

}
```

Step 4: Running the Application

With the model and controller in place, you can now run
the application. Navigate to the project directory and
execute:

```bash
./gradlew run
```

This command starts the Micronaut server, and the REST

91

API is now accessible at

`http://localhost:8080/books`. You can use tools like Postman or cURL to test the API. ### Step 5: Testing the API

List Books:

```bash
curl http://localhost:8080/books
```

You should receive an empty list `[]`.

Add a Book:

```bash
curl -X POST http://localhost:8080/books -H "Content-Type: application/json" -d '{"id":"1","title":"The Great Gatsby","author":"F. Scott Fitzgerald"}'
```

This should return the added book.

List Books Again:

Check the list of books to see if the new book has been added.

```bash
curl http://localhost:8080/books
```

Step 6: Utilizing Dependency Injection

One of the strengths of Micronaut is its robust support for dependency injection. Let's enhance our API by adding a service to manage the business logic. Create a new file named `BookService.groovy`.

```groovy
package        example.micronaut.books        import
javax.inject.Singleton

@Singleton

class BookService {


private List<Book> bookList = []

List<Book> list() { return bookList

}

Book save(Book book) { bookList.add(book) return book

}

}
```

Now, modify the `BookController` to use `BookService`:

```groovy
import io.micronaut.http.annotation.Controller  import
io.micronaut.http.annotation.Get                import
io.micronaut.http.annotation.Post               import
io.micronaut.http.annotation.Body               import
javax.inject.Inject

@Controller("/books") class BookController {

@Inject

BookService bookService
```

```
@Get("/") List<Book> list() {
return bookService.list()
}
@Post("/")
Book    save(@Body    Book    book)    {    return
bookService.save(book)
}
}
```
` ` `

We started with a brief introduction to Micronaut, discussed the benefits of using it, and went through the steps to set up a basic microservice framework. By using Micronaut's features such as compile-time dependency injection and seamless cloud integration, developers can create resilient and performant microservices remarkably efficiently.

Introduction to Micronaut and Its Advantages

With the advent of microservices architecture and the growing demand for cloud-native applications, developers are constantly on the lookout for tools and frameworks that can help them build efficient systems with minimal overhead. One such framework that has gained significant traction in the Java ecosystem is Micronaut.

1.1 What is Micronaut?

Micronaut is a modern, JVM-based framework designed

for building microservices and serverless applications. It was created by Object Computing, Inc. (OCI) and is tailored for rapid development, low memory consumption, and fast startup times. Unlike traditional frameworks like Spring, Micronaut does not rely on runtime reflection and heavy classpath scanning. Instead, it utilizes a compile-time dependency injection approach, which leads to less overhead and enhanced performance.

Micronaut supports multiple programming languages, including Java, Kotlin, and Groovy, making it a versatile choice for developers who prefer to work in different environments. Its combination of simplicity, speed, and a rich feature set has made it an attractive option for developers looking to adopt a microservices approach.

1.2 Advantages of Using Micronaut in Groovy ### 1.2.1 Seamless Integration with Groovy

For developers who are accustomed to the Groovy programming language, Micronaut offers seamless integration that leverages Groovy's dynamic features and syntax simplifications. You can write concise and expressive code while still benefiting from Micronaut's powerful features like annotation-based configuration, dependency injection, and AOP (Aspect-Oriented Programming). This synergy allows developers to focus on delivering functionality rather than boilerplate code.

1.2.2 Compile-Time Dependency Injection

One of the standout features of Micronaut is its compile-time dependency injection. Unlike many frameworks that rely on runtime reflection, Micronaut processes annotations at compile time, resulting in faster startup times and reduced memory consumption. This is particularly beneficial for Groovy developers, who can take advantage of the language's flexible syntax while enjoying the performance benefits that Micronaut provides.

1.2.3 Low Memory Footprint

Micronaut is designed to be lightweight, with a focus on minimizing the memory footprint of applications. This is especially important in cloud-native architectures where resources can be constrained or costly. The efficient memory management achieved through compile-time processing makes Micronaut applications ideal for developing microservices that are often deployed in environments where every byte of memory counts.

1.2.4 Built-In Support for Reactive Programming

In today's development landscape, reactive programming has gained prominence as a means to build responsive and resilient applications. Micronaut has built-in support for reactive programming paradigms through its integration with Project Reactor and RxJava. Developers using Groovy can leverage these libraries to create asynchronous, non-blocking applications that can handle a large number of concurrent users with ease.

1.2.5 Microservices Ready

Micronaut has microservice architecture at its core, providing support for the creation and deployment of lightweight microservices. With features like service discovery, distributed tracing, and API gateway integration, developers can efficiently create a network of interacting services. Using Groovy with Micronaut allows for quick prototyping and development of robust services that can be easily orchestrated in a larger system.

1.2.6 Easy Testing and Mocking

Testing is an integral part of software development. Micronaut's design emphasizes testability, with built-in support for various testing frameworks and tools. Developers can easily create unit tests and integration tests for their Groovy applications using libraries like Spock or JUnit. Micronaut's mocking capabilities also make it easy to simulate dependencies during testing, resulting in faster development cycles and improved code quality.

1.2.7 Rich Ecosystem and Community Support

Being a part of the JVM ecosystem, Micronaut benefits from a rich pool of libraries and tools. Its growing community contributes to a vast array of plugins and extensions, enabling developers to enhance their applications with minimal effort. Furthermore, Micronaut's official documentation and community forums provide ample resources for troubleshooting and learning.

As organizations continue to adopt microservices and cloud-native strategies, the need for frameworks that simplify the development and deployment of applications becomes ever more critical. Micronaut stands out as a frontrunner in this space—especially for Groovy developers—offering a powerful combination of performance, flexibility, and ease of use. With its emphasis on compile-time processing, low memory usage, and support for reactive programming, Micronaut empowers developers to create efficient applications that meet the demands of modern software development.

Creating Scalable Microservices Using Micronaut

This chapter explores how to build scalable microservices using Micronaut, a modern framework designed for building microservices and serverless applications with a focus on minimal memory consumption and fast startup times. We will utilize Groovy in this chapter to demonstrate the simplicity and elegance of developing microservices.

What is Micronaut?

Micronaut is a JVM-based framework that provides a powerful and lightweight solution for building modular applications. Unlike traditional Java frameworks that rely heavily on reflection and runtime configuration, Micronaut leverages ahead-of-time (AOT) compilation and dependency injection, greatly improving startup performance and scalability. Its architecture is designed for cloud-native applications, making it an excellent choice for deploying microservices in environments such as Kubernetes or serverless platforms.

Why Use Groovy?

Groovy is a dynamic language for the JVM that integrates seamlessly with Java. It's known for its concise syntax and powerful features, including closures, dynamic typing, and a rich set of libraries. Using Groovy with Micronaut allows developers to create microservices quickly while benefiting from Groovy's expressive syntax.

Setting Up Your Environment

Before diving into code, ensure you have the following installed:

Java JDK 11 or higher: Micronaut runs on the Java Virtual Machine; therefore, a compatible JDK is necessary.

Groovy: We'll be using Groovy to implement our services.

Micronaut CLI: This tool simplifies the creation and management of Micronaut projects. ### Installation Steps

Install Java: Make sure you have Java installed by running:

```bash
java -version
```

Install Groovy: You can download Groovy from [the official website](https://groovy-lang.org/download.html) or use SDKMAN:

```bash
curl -s get.sdkman.io | bash
source "$HOME/.sdkman/bin/sdkman-init.sh" sdk install groovy
```

Install Micronaut: To install the Micronaut CLI, use SDKMAN as well:

```bash
sdk install micronaut
```

```
```

Creating a Simple Microservice ### Step 1: Initialize a New Project

Use the Micronaut CLI to create a new project. We'll create a simple "Book Inventory" service.

```bash

mn create-app com.example.bookinventory --lang=groovy
cd bookinventory
```

This command generates a basic Micronaut project structure for us. ### Step 2: Define the Domain Model

In your `src/main/groovy/com/example/bookinventory` directory, create a new file called `Book.groovy` with the following content:

```groovy

package com.example.bookinventory

import io.micronaut.core.annotation.Introspected
@Introspected

class Book { String id String title String author String isbn

Book(String id, String title, String author, String isbn) {
this.id = id

this.title = title this.author = author this.isbn = isbn

}

}
```

Step 3: Create a Controller
100

Controllers in Micronaut handle the incoming HTTP requests. Create `BookController.groovy`:

```groovy
package         com.example.bookinventory      import
io.micronaut.http.annotation.*                  import
javax.inject.Singleton

@Singleton @Controller("/books") class BookController {

private List<Book> books = []


@Get("/") List<Book> list() {

return books

}

@Post("/")

Book save(@Body Book book) { books.add(book)

return book

}

}
```

In this controller, we provide two endpoints: one for listing all books and another for adding a new book. We use a simple in-memory list to store our books.

Step 4: Run the Application

To run the application, use the following command:

```bash
./gradlew run
```

```
```

You should see something like this in your terminal, indicating that the application has started:

```
```

Application 'bookinventory' is running at http://localhost:8080

```
```

Step 5: Testing the Microservice

You can test your microservice using tools like `curl` or Postman.

Add a New Book:

```bash
curl -X POST http://localhost:8080/books -H "Content-Type: application/json" -d '{"id":"1", "title":"The Great Gatsby", "author":"F. Scott Fitzgerald", "isbn":"9780743273565"}'
```

List All Books:

```bash
curl http://localhost:8080/books
```

Enhancing Scalability

While the current implementation provides a basic microservice, scalability considerations are crucial. Here are a few strategies to enhance scalability:

1. External Data Store

In a real-world application, you'd likely use an external database (e.g., PostgreSQL or MongoDB) instead of an in-memory list for data persistence. Micronaut provides support for various databases and ORM libraries, allowing you to easily integrate them into your application.

2. API Gateway

In a microservices architecture, an API Gateway can manage requests to different services. Consider implementing an API Gateway using tools like Kong or Spring Cloud Gateway to route requests to different microservices.

3. Dockerize Your Microservice

Containerizing your microservice using Docker facilitates deployment and scaling. Here's a basic Dockerfile for the `bookinventory` application:

```dockerfile
FROM adoptopenjdk:11-jre

COPY        build/libs/bookinventory-*.jar        app.jar
ENTRYPOINT ["java", "-jar", "/app.jar"]
```

To build your Docker image, run:

```bash
docker build -t bookinventory .
```

Now, you can deploy your service in any Kubernetes cluster or cloud provider.

In this chapter, we explored the capabilities of Micronaut

for building scalable microservices in Groovy. We created a simple book inventory service, learned how to set up a project, and implemented basic CRUD functionalities. By leveraging Micronaut's architecture, we can build applications that are lightweight, fast, and scalable—perfect for modern cloud-native environments.

Chapter 7: Authentication and Security in Groovy Backends

This chapter focuses on the core principles of authentication and security in Groovy backend development, examining best practices, frameworks, and tools available to developers.

7.1 The Importance of Authentication

Authentication is the process by which an application verifies the identity of a user. It is the first line of defense against unauthorized access and sets the foundation for user trust. In Groovy backend development, understanding the various mechanisms available for authentication is critical.

Types of Authentication

Basic Authentication: This is a straightforward mechanism where users provide a username and password. While easy to implement, it is not suitable for secure applications without additional protections such as HTTPS.

Token-Based Authentication: More advanced than basic authentication, this involves generating a token upon user login. The token is then sent with each subsequent request, allowing the server to authenticate the user without needing to revalidate credentials.

OAuth and OpenID Connect: These protocols provide means for third-party authentication. They allow users to log in with credentials from platforms like Google or Facebook and are particularly useful for applications that want to leverage existing user accounts without managing extensive user data.

Multi-Factor Authentication (MFA): This adds an additional layer of security by requiring users to provide two or more verification factors, making it harder for unauthorized users to gain access.

7.2 Implementing Authentication in Groovy

When developing a Groovy backend, several frameworks can assist with implementing authentication. The most notable ones include Spring Security and Grails Security.

Spring Security

Spring Security is a powerful and customizable authentication and access-control framework for Java applications, including those written in Groovy.

Configuration: Spring Security's XML or Java-based configuration allows developers to define security rules, including which endpoints require authentication and which do not.

User Details Service: By implementing the UserDetailsService interface, developers can customize how user details are retrieved, enabling backend integration with databases or other user storage solutions.

Password Encoding: Implementing strong password policies is vital. Spring Security provides various password encoders to ensure that passwords are stored securely.

Grails Security

For developers using the Grails framework, Grails Security plugins can simplify the implementation of authentication:

Easy Integration: Grails provides plugins that seamlessly integrate authentication and authorization features into applications, dramatically reducing the amount of boilerplate code required.

Role-based Access Control: Grails plugins support role-based access control out of the box, allowing developers to define user roles and permissions easily.

Customizable Forms: Grails allows for customizable login forms that can be tailored to fit the design of the application while maintaining security best practices.

7.3 Security Best Practices

Developers must prioritize security to protect sensitive user data and maintain application integrity. Here are essential security best practices when developing Groovy backends:

Use HTTPS: Always use HTTPS to encrypt data in transit. This is critical for preventing man-in-the- middle attacks and ensuring data integrity.

Input Validation: Implement robust input validation to prevent injection attacks (like SQL or script injections). Use libraries like Hibernate Validator when validating incoming data.

Error Handling: Avoid exposing sensitive information through error messages. Implement generic error messages that do not disclose whether the input was invalid due to incorrect credentials or other reasons.

Session Management: Properly manage user sessions.

Set sensible timeouts and provide means for logging out users. Invalidating sessions after logout is crucial to prevent session hijacking.

Rate Limiting: Implement rate limiting to protect against brute force attacks. This can be done at the application or API gateway level to restrict the number of attempts a user can make to log in.

Regular Security Audits: Conduct regular security audits and update libraries and frameworks to the latest versions to mitigate known vulnerabilities.

Documentation and Training: Documentation of security practices and proper training for developers on secure coding practices are essential to maintain a security-focused development culture.

7.4 Security Testing

To ensure the effectiveness of authentication practices and overall application security, implementing a robust security testing strategy is essential:

Static Analysis: Use static code analysis tools to identify potential vulnerabilities in the code before deployment.

Penetration Testing: Conduct penetration testing to simulate attacks on the system and identify weaknesses.

Automated Testing: Incorporate automated security tests in the CI/CD pipeline to ensure that code merging does not introduce new vulnerabilities.

As we advance into an era where data breaches and cyber threats continue to proliferate, prioritizing authentication and security in Groovy backend development is essential.

By leveraging the right frameworks, adhering to best practices, and maintaining vigilant testing and monitoring, developers can build secure applications that users can trust. The significance of a well-thought-out approach to authentication and security in software development cannot be overstated, as it forms the backbone of user confidence and data protection in the digital age.

Implementing Secure Authentication Mechanisms

Authentication mechanisms are a key component in safeguarding web applications against unauthorized access and cyber threats. Groovy, a powerful and dynamic language for the Java platform, is widely used in backend development, particularly with frameworks like Grails. This chapter will provide an overview of implementing secure authentication mechanisms in Groovy, discussing best practices, techniques, and practical examples to help developers fortify their applications.

Understanding Authentication and Its Importance

Authentication is the process of verifying the identity of a user, system, or entity. It ensures that only authorized users have access to particular resources within an application. Secure authentication mechanisms help to protect sensitive data and maintain user trust. The various types of authentication methods include:

Traditional username and password: The most common form, where users enter credentials to access a system.

Multi-factor authentication (MFA): Adds an additional layer of security by requiring more than one form of verification, such as a text message or authentication app.

OAuth/OpenID Connect: Enables third-party applications to grant limited access to user accounts.

JWT (JSON Web Tokens): A compact, URL-safe way to represent claims to be transferred between two parties.

In this chapter, we will focus primarily on the implementation of traditional username/password authentication, MFA, and JWT-based authentication.

Setting Up a Groovy Environment

Before diving into implementation, ensure you have a Groovy environment set up. You can use Groovy with the Grails framework for ease of development. Follow these steps to set up your environment:

Install Groovy: Download and install Groovy from the official website or use SDKMAN.

Create a Grails project: Use the Grails command-line tool to generate a new project.

```bash
grails create-app secure-auth-app cd secure-auth-app
```

Add dependencies: Include necessary dependencies for secure authentication in your `build.gradle` file. For example, you might add Spring Security for managing authentication and authorization.

```groovy
dependencies {

compile   'org.springframework.boot:spring-boot-starter-security' compile 'io.jsonwebtoken:jjwt:0.9.1' // For JWT handling

// Other necessary dependencies

}
```

Implementing Username and Password Authentication

User Entity: Define a User domain class to map users to your database.

```groovy
class User {

String username String password String email

static constraints = {

username unique: true, blank: false, size: 5..15 password blank: false, size: 8..100

email email: true, unique: true

}
}
```

User Registration: Create a registration controller to handle user signup. Ensure passwords are hashed before storing them in the database.

```groovy
class UserController {
```

```groovy
def springSecurityService
def register() {
def user = new User(params)
user.password                                      =
springSecurityService.encodePassword(user.password)  if
(user.save(flush: true)) {
// Registration successful
} else {
// Handle registration errors
}
}
}
```

Authentication: Use Grails' Spring Security plugin to configure authentication. Adjust your

`application.groovy` to enable security settings.

```groovy
grails.plugin.springsecurity.userLookup.userDomainClass
Name                   =                   'com.myapp.User'
grails.plugin.springsecurity.userLookup.authorityJoinClas
sName              =               'com.myapp.UserRole'
grails.plugin.springsecurity.controllerAnnotations.staticR
ules = [

[pattern: '/login/**', access: ['permitAll']],

[pattern: '/**', access: ['IS_AUTHENTICATED_FULLY']]
]
```

```
```

Implementing Multi-Factor Authentication (MFA)

To enhance security, implementing MFA can be a powerful tool. This approach typically involves sending a one-time passcode (OTP) to the user's email or phone.

Generate OTP: When a user attempts to log in, generate an OTP and send it to their registered email or phone.

```groovy
def sendOtp(String email) {

String otp = UUID.randomUUID().toString().substring(0, 6) // For simplicity

// Send OTP to email logic return otp

}
```

Verify OTP: After the user enters their OTP, verify it before granting access.

```groovy
def verifyOtp(String enteredOtp, String sessionOtp) {
return enteredOtp == sessionOtp

}
```

Update User Controller: Modify the login flow in your UserController to include OTP verification. ## Implementing JWT-Based Authentication

JWTs are widely recognized for their ease of use in

stateless authentication. Implementing JWT involves token generation upon user login and secured routes that require token validation.

Token Generation: Generate a JWT when a user successfully logs in.

```groovy
def generateToken(User user) { String jwt = Jwts.builder()
.setSubject(user.username)
.setExpiration(new Date(System.currentTimeMillis() + 86400000)) // 1 day
.signWith(SignatureAlgorithm.HS512, 'secretKey')
.compact() return jwt
}
```

Token Validation: Create a filter to validate JWTs in incoming requests.

```groovy
class JwtAuthenticationFilter extends GenericFilterBean {
@Override
void doFilter(ServletRequest request, ServletResponse response, FilterChain chain) throws IOException, ServletException {
String token = getTokenFromRequest((HttpServletRequest) request) if (token != null && validateToken(token)) {
Authentication auth = getAuthentication(token)
```

SecurityContextHolder.getContext().setAuthentication(aut
h)

}

chain.doFilter(request, response)

}

}
```

**Configure Security**: Finally, configure your
`SecurityConfig` to use the JWT filter.

```groovy @Configuration @EnableWebSecurity

class              SecurityConfig              extends
WebSecurityConfigurerAdapter { @Autowired

private JwtAuthenticationFilter jwtAuthenticationFilter

@Override

protected void configure(HttpSecurity http) throws
Exception { http

.csrf().disable()

.sessionManagement().sessionCreationPolicy(SessionCreat
ionPolicy.STATELESS)

.and()

.addFilterBefore(jwtAuthenticationFilter,
UsernamePasswordAuthenticationFilter.class)

}

}

```
```

In this chapter, we explored the implementation of secure authentication mechanisms in Groovy, focusing on username and password authentication, multi-factor authentication, and JWT-based authentication. By following best practices, developers can effectively enhance the security of their applications, protecting sensitive user data and building user trust.

Managing Authorization and User Roles

In modern web applications, managing user access and roles is crucial for maintaining security and ensuring that users have the appropriate permissions to perform specific actions. Groovy, a powerful dynamic language for the Java platform, integrates seamlessly with popular frameworks such as Grails and Spring, making it a suitable choice for backend development. This chapter will explore strategies and best practices for managing authorization and user roles in Groovy, providing insights into implementing robust security measures within your applications.

Understanding Roles and Permissions

Before diving into implementation, it's essential to understand the concepts of roles and permissions.

Roles are labels assigned to users that define a set of permissions. They are often used to categorize users based on their function in the application (e.g., admin, editor, viewer).

Permissions are specific actions that users can perform (e.g., create, read, update, delete). These actions can be independently assigned to roles.

Role-Based Access Control (RBAC)

Role-Based Access Control (RBAC) is a widely used access control mechanism that associates permissions with roles rather than individual users. This approach simplifies permission management, making it easier to modify user access by changing their roles rather than their individual permissions.

Implementing User Roles in Groovy ### 1. Setting Up the Environment

Ensure that you have a Groovy environment set up, preferably using a web framework like Grails or Spring Boot. These frameworks offer features to manage user sessions and integrate security with minimal effort.

2. Defining User and Role Models

To manage roles and permissions efficiently, you should define user and role models in your domain classes. Here's an example using Groovy:

```groovy
class User {

String username String password Set<Role> roles

static hasMany = [roles: Role] // A user can have multiple roles static constraints = {

username blank: false, unique: true password blank: false

}
```

```
}

class Role {
String authority // e.g., ROLE_ADMIN, ROLE_USER
static constraints = {
authority blank: false, unique: true
}
}
```

3. Establishing a Relationship Between Users and Roles

You can use a many-to-many relationship to establish how users and roles associate with each other. In the User class, we've indicated that a user can have multiple roles. Similarly, a role can be assigned to multiple users.

4. Using a Security Framework

Integrating a security framework is critical for managing authentication and authorization processes. Spring Security is a popular choice in the Groovy ecosystem:

a. Configuration

Configure Spring Security by adding necessary dependencies in your `build.gradle` file:

```groovy
dependencies {
implementation 'org.springframework.boot:spring-boot-starter-security'                                 implementation 'org.springframework.security:spring-security-config'
```

```
}
```

b. Security Configuration

Create a security configuration class to specify user roles and permissions:

```groovy
import org.springframework.context.annotation.Bean

import org.springframework.security.config.annotation.web.builders.HttpSecurity

import org.springframework.security.config.annotation.web.configuration.EnableWebSecurity

import org.springframework.security.config.annotation.web.configuration.WebSecurityConfigurerAdapter

@EnableWebSecurity

class SecurityConfig extends WebSecurityConfigurerAdapter { @Override

protected void configure(HttpSecurity http) throws Exception { http

.authorizeRequests()

.antMatchers('/admin/**').hasRole('ADMIN')

.antMatchers('/uscr/**').hasAnyRole('USER', 'ADMIN')

.antMatchers('/', '/login').permitAll()

.anyRequest().authenticated()
```

```
.and()
.formLogin()
.loginPage('/login')

.permitAll()
.and()
.logout()
.permitAll()
}
}
```
` ` `

In this configuration example, we restrict access to certain endpoints based on roles. Admins have access to

`/admin/**`, while both Users and Admins can access `/user/**`, and everyone can access the login page. ### 5. Handling Authentication

You will need to provide a mechanism to authenticate users. This can be accomplished using in-memory authentication for a simple setup or by integrating a database for user information:

` ` `groovy @Override

protected void configure(AuthenticationManagerBuilder auth) throws Exception { auth.jdbcAuthentication()

.dataSource(dataSource)

.usersByUsernameQuery("SELECT username, password, enabled FROM users WHERE username=?")

```
.authoritiesByUsernameQuery("SELECT      username,
authority FROM user_roles WHERE username=?");
}
```
```

### 6. User Registration and Role Assignment

A crucial part of the application is allowing users to register with specific roles. Create a registration form where admin users can assign roles during user creation.

```groovy
def register(UserCommand cmd) {

def user = new User(username: cmd.username, password:
cmd.password)
user.addToRoles(Role.findByAuthority('ROLE_USER'))
// Assign default role user.save(flush: true)

}
```

You can adjust the roles based on your application logic, such as allowing admins to assign other roles. ## Testing Role Management

Testing your role and authorization management is essential. Ensure to write unit tests to check permission accuracy and authorization flows. Using Groovy's built-in testing capabilities or frameworks like Spock can streamline your testing process.

```groovy
class UserRoleSpec extends Specification {

def "test role assignment"() { given: "A new user"
```
```

```groovy
def user = new User(username: 'testUser', password:
'pass123').save()

def role = new Role(authority: 'ROLE_USER').save()
when: "Assigning a role" user.addToRoles(role)

then: "User should have the role assigned"
user.roles.contains(role)
}
}
```
```

By leveraging Groovy's capabilities and integrating with powerful frameworks like Spring Security, you can create secure applications that effectively manage user access. As users and roles grow in complexity, consistently revisiting and refining your authorization strategy will lead to a more secure and manageable application environment.
```

Chapter 8: Database Integration in Groovy

As applications become increasingly data-driven, effective database integration is essential for backend development. Groovy, a powerful language built on the Java platform, provides a versatile and expressive syntax that simplifies data handling and integration tasks. This chapter will explore how to seamlessly integrate databases into Groovy applications, focusing on popular databases, ORM frameworks, and best practices.

8.1 Understanding Groovy and Databases

Groovy inherits Java's robustness while offering a more compact syntax, making it an ideal choice for developing backend services. Databases serve as the backbone of most applications, storing critical data and allowing for retrieval, manipulation, and management.

In Groovy, you can connect to various databases using JDBC (Java Database Connectivity), Groovy's built- in support for SQL, or through the use of Object Relational Mapping (ORM) frameworks like GORM or Hibernate.

8.2 Setting Up Your Database Environment

Before diving into the code, ensure that you have a reliable database set up. For this chapter, we can choose between:

MySQL: A popular open-source relational database management system.

PostgreSQL: An advanced open-source relational database known for its robustness.

H2: An in-memory database ideal for development

and testing. ### 8.2.1 Installing MySQL

To use MySQL as your database, follow these steps:

Download and Install MySQL from the official website.

Create a Database: Once installed, log in to the MySQL shell and create a new database with the command:

```sql
CREATE DATABASE groovy_example;
```

Create a User: It's a good practice to create a specific user for your application:

```sql
CREATE USER 'groovy_user'@'localhost' IDENTIFIED BY 'password';
GRANT ALL PRIVILEGES ON groovy_example.* TO 'groovy_user'@'localhost';
```

Connect to your database: Use your preferred IDE or database management tool to connect. ### 8.2.2 Configure Your Groovy Application

Ensure you include the necessary dependencies in your `build.gradle` file or `pom.xml` if you're using Maven. For Gradle, add:

```groovy
dependencies {
```

```
implementation          'org.grails:grails-datastore-gorm-
hibernate5:7.0.0'   runtime   'mysql:mysql-connector-
java:8.0.23'
}
```
` ` `

8.3 Using GORM for Database Interaction

GORM (Grails Object Relational Mapping) is a powerful and convenient ORM framework for Groovy, providing an easy way to interact with databases.

8.3.1 Creating Domain Classes

To start, create domain classes that represent your database tables. For example, if you are building a simple application to manage books, create a class like this:

` ` `groovy class Book {

String title String author

Date publicationDate

static constraints = {

title blank: false, maxSize: 255 author blank: false, maxSize: 255 publicationDate nullable: true

}

}
` ` `

8.3.2 Performing CRUD Operations

GORM simplifies the Create, Read, Update, and Delete (CRUD) operations. Below are some examples: #### Creating a New Record

125

```groovy
def newBook = new Book(title: "Groovy in Action", author:
"Dierk    König",    publicationDate:    new    Date())
newBook.save(flush: true)
```

Retrieving Records

```groovy
def allBooks = Book.list()

def specificBook = Book.findByTitle("Groovy in Action")
```

Updating a Record

```groovy
specificBook.author    =    "Dierk    König    and    others"
specificBook.save(flush: true)
```

Deleting a Record

```groovy specificBook.delete(flush: true)
```

8.3.3 Running Database Migrations

When working on multi-developer projects, maintaining
database schema consistency is vital. Use GORM's
migration capabilities or additional tools like Liquibase or
Flyway for managing changes.

8.4 Native SQL Queries

While GORM provides a high-level abstraction, sometimes

126

you may need to execute native SQL queries. This is easily done with:

```groovy
def sql = """SELECT * FROM book WHERE author = :author""" def results = Book.executeQuery(sql, [author: "Dierk König"])
```

8.5 Handling Transactions

Groovy provides support for handling transactions, ensuring data integrity. Use the `withTransaction` method to manage transactions effectively:

```groovy
Book.withTransaction { status -> try {

newBook.save(flush: true)

// Additional operations

} catch (Exception e) { status.setRollbackOnly()

}

}
```

8.6 Best Practices for Database Integration

Use Connection Pools: Use connection pooling libraries like HikariCP for efficient database connections.

Validate Input: Always validate input before saving to the database to prevent issues like SQL injection.

Employ DTOs: Use Data Transfer Objects to separate your domain model from the data sent over the network.

Optimize Queries: Analyze and optimize your queries to ensure performance remains high, especially under load.

Use Database Migrations: Always manage database schema changes in a structured way to prevent inconsistencies.

Integrating a database into a Groovy application can seem daunting, but with frameworks like GORM and robust support for SQL queries, the process becomes much more manageable. By following best practices and utilizing Groovy's features effectively, developers can create powerful, data-centric applications with ease. As we continue to build more complex applications, mastering these integration techniques will be invaluable. In the next chapter, we will explore the deployment strategies for Groovy applications, ensuring our backend services run smoothly in production environments.

Connecting to Databases with GORM

GORM (Grails Object Relational Mapping) is a powerful object relational mapping tool built on top of Groovy, providing a seamless and efficient way to interact with relational databases. This chapter will guide you through the process of setting up GORM in your Groovy applications, connecting to various databases, and performing basic CRUD (Create, Read, Update, Delete) operations.

Understanding GORM

GORM simplifies the database interaction by allowing developers to interact with databases using Groovy objects. It abstracts the complexities of SQL and lets you work with high-level domain objects. GORM supports a variety of database systems, such as MySQL, PostgreSQL, and Oracle, making it versatile for many projects.

Key Features of GORM

Simplicity: GORM eliminates the boilerplate code required for database access.

Dynamic Finders: GORM provides dynamic methods for querying the database without writing SQL.

Seamless Integration: Integrates easily within Grails and Groovy applications.

Transaction Management: Built-in support for transactions to ensure data integrity.

Validation: Supports data validation using Groovy's built-in features. ## Setting Up GORM in a Groovy Application

Step 1: Create a Groovy Project

You can create a Groovy project using either a Grails application or a simple Groovy application. For this example, we'll set up a basic Groovy application.

Ensure you have Groovy installed. Use the following command to create a new Groovy project:

```bash
mkdir MyGormProject cd MyGormProject
```

```
```

Step 2: Add GORM Dependencies

Depending on the build tool you are using, you need to add the GORM dependencies. If you are using Gradle, add the following lines to your `build.gradle` file:

```groovy
dependencies {
```

implementation 'org.grails:gorm-hibernate5:7.0.0' // Use the latest version implementation 'org.hibernate:hibernate-core:5.4.30.Final' implementation 'org.grails.plugins:hibernate5:7.0.0'

runtimeOnly 'mysql:mysql-connector-java:8.0.XX' // Replace XX with the latest version

}

```
```

Step 3: Configure Database Connection

Next, configure the database connection by creating a `DataSource.groovy` file in the `src/main/resources` directory:

```groovy
dataSource {
```

pooled = true

driverClassName = 'com.mysql.cj.jdbc.Driver'

dialect = 'org.hibernate.dialect.MySQL5InnoDBDialect' username = 'your_username'

password = 'your_password'

dbCreate = 'update' // options: 'create', 'create-drop',

'update',   'validate'   url   =
'jdbc:mysql://localhost:3306/your_database'
}
```

Make sure to replace `your_username`, `your_password`, and `your_database` with your actual database credentials and name.

### Step 4: Create Domain Classes

Domain classes represent the tables in your database. Create a new Groovy class for your domain object. For example, create a `Book` class:

```groovy class Book {
String title String author
Date publishedDate
static constraints = {
title nullable: false, blank: false author nullable: false, blank: false publishedDate nullable: true
}
}
```

In this class, `constraints` define the rules that validate the data. ## Performing CRUD Operations

With GORM set up, you can now perform CRUD operations on your domain classes. ### Creating Records

To create a new record in the database, you can use the `save()` method:
```

```groovy
def book = new Book(title: 'The Great Gatsby', author: 'F.
Scott Fitzgerald', publishedDate: new Date())
book.save(flush: true)
```

The `flush: true` argument ensures that the data is
immediately inserted into the database.

Reading Records

To fetch records from the database, use dynamic finders:

```groovy
def books = Book.findAllByAuthor('F. Scott Fitzgerald')
books.each { println it.title }
```

You can also retrieve a single record using `get()`:

```groovy
def book = Book.get(1)
println "Title: ${book.title}, Author: ${book.author}"
```

Updating Records

To update an existing record, retrieve it first, make your
changes, and then save:

```groovy
def book = Book.get(1)
book.title = 'The Great Gatsby - Updated' book.save(flush:
```

true)
```

### Deleting Records

To delete a record, use the `delete()` method:

```groovy
def book = Book.get(1) book.delete(flush: true)
```

Advanced Features ### Transactions

GORM supports transactions, allowing you to group several database operations into a single transaction. You can use the `withTransaction` method:

```groovy
Book.withTransaction { status -> try {

def book = new Book(title: '1984', author: 'George Orwell') book.save(flush: true)

// Perform more operations

} catch (Exception e) {

status.setRollbackOnly() // Rollback the transaction on error

}

}
```

Querying with HQL
```

For more complex queries, you can use Hibernate Query Language (HQL):

```groovy
def results = Book.executeQuery("FROM Book WHERE author = :author", [author: 'F. Scott Fitzgerald'])
results.each { println it.title }
```

Connecting to databases with GORM in Groovy dramatically simplifies the process of managing database interactions in backend development. This chapter covered the fundamentals of setting up GORM, connecting to a database, and performing basic CRUD operations. As you continue to develop your application, take advantage of GORM's advanced features to build robust and efficient data-driven applications. The combination of Groovy and GORM offers a powerful toolkit for modern web development.

Handling Queries and Transactions Effectively

One of the critical functionalities required in any backend system is the ability to handle queries and transactions efficiently. Groovy, a powerful language that runs on the Java Virtual Machine (JVM), offers developers powerful tools and libraries to manage database interactions seamlessly. This chapter will delve into best practices for handling queries and transactions in Groovy, providing insights into leveraging the language's features and ecosystem.

1. Understanding the Basics of Groovy and GORM

Groovy is a dynamic language that integrates seamlessly with Java, enabling developers to utilize existing Java libraries while benefiting from Groovy's concise syntax and features. In the context of database interactions, Groovy Object-Relational Mapping (GORM) is a key library that simplifies the process of database access and manipulation.

1.1. Introduction to GORM

GORM is a powerful ORM framework that allows you to work with databases in a more intuitive and

object-oriented manner. Built on top of Hibernate, GORM reduces the amount of boilerplate code needed for CRUD (Create, Read, Update, Delete) operations while providing advanced features such as caching, automatic validation, and support for complex queries.

To get started with GORM, you need to define your domain classes, which represent the tables in your database. Here's a simple example of a domain class in Groovy:

```groovy
class Book {
```

String title String author

Date publishedDate

static constraints = {

titlc blank: false, maxSize: 255 author blank: false publishedDate nullable: true

}

```
}
```

In this example, the `Book` class has three properties, each with associated constraints that help enforce data integrity at the database level.

2. Writing Efficient Queries

When it comes to querying data, performance is key. GORM provides various ways to retrieve data, from simple finders to dynamic queries.

2.1. Using GORM Query Methods

GORM offers several built-in query methods to simplify data retrieval. You can find records by specific attributes using methods like `findBy`, `findAllBy`, and others. For example:

```groovy
def book = Book.findByTitle("Groovy in Action") def allBooks = Book.findAllByAuthor("Scott Davis")
```

These methods are powerful yet easy to read, promoting clarity in your code. ### 2.2. Dynamic Finders

Dynamic finders are another feature of GORM that allows you to construct queries based on property names. They are automatically created based on the properties of your domain classes:

```groovy
def                         books                         =
```

```
Book.findAllByPublishedDateBetween(startDate,
endDate)
```
```
```

Dynamic finders help you create flexible queries with minimal code, but keep performance in mind—overusing them can lead to inefficient queries.

2.3. Criteria Queries

For more complex queries, Groovy offers Criteria queries, which allow you to specify conditions programatically. This is particularly useful for dynamic and conditional queries:

```groovy
def books = Book.createCriteria().list { eq("author", "Scott
Davis") ge("publishedDate", new Date() - 365)

}
```
```
```

Using criteria can yield not only better performance but also clearer intent in your code. ## 3. Managing Transactions

Transactions are essential for ensuring data integrity, especially when multiple operations need to succeed or fail together. GORM provides built-in transaction management that simplifies the handling of transactions.

3.1. Using `withTransaction`

The `withTransaction` method allows you to define transactional blocks of code:

```groovy
```

```
Book.withTransaction { status -> try {

def book = new Book(title: "Learning Groovy", author:
"John Doe") book.save(flush: true)

// Additional operations can go here

} catch (Exception e) { status.setRollbackOnly()

// Handle exception

}

}


```

In this example, if any operation within the
`withTransaction` block fails, all changes will be rolled
back, preserving the integrity of your database.

3.2. Handling Exceptions

Error management is vital within transactions. Always
encapsulate your transaction logic in try-catch blocks and
handle exceptions gracefully. Logging and providing
meaningful feedback to your users should also be
prioritized.

3.3. Transaction Propagation

Understanding transaction propagation is crucial,
especially in complex systems. GORM allows you to define
how transactions behave when methods are called
internally. You can define propagation rules such as
`REQUIRED`, `REQUIRES_NEW`, etc., to manage
complex transactional scenarios.

4. Performance Optimization

While Groovy and GORM are designed to make development easier, it's important to keep performance in mind. Here are some tips to optimize your database interactions:

4.1. Eager vs. Lazy Loading

Understand the difference between eager and lazy loading when dealing with associations. Eager loading retrieves related objects immediately, while lazy loading retrieves them only when accessed. Use them according to your application needs.

4.2. Pagination and Sorting

When dealing with large datasets, utilize pagination and sorting methods provided by GORM to enhance user experience and reduce loading times:

```groovy
def books = Book.list(params)
```

4.3. Avoiding N+1 Queries

Be aware of the "N+1 query" problem where fetching a list of items, each with its related objects, can lead to an excessive number of queries. Optimize your database interactions by using `eager fetching` for necessary relationships.

By leveraging Groovy's robust features, developers can create clean, efficient, and maintainable code that interacts seamlessly with their databases. As you continue to explore and deepen your knowledge of Groovy and its ecosystem, you will find that crafting powerful backend solutions becomes an increasingly fluent and satisfying endeavor.

Chapter 9: Advanced API Development

As digital ecosystems evolve, the demand for advanced API development has surged, necessitating a strategic and informed approach. In this chapter, we will delve into the intricacies of advanced API development, covering key concepts, best practices, and modern tools that enhance backend development.

9.1 Understanding API Basics and Importance

Before diving into advanced topics, it's essential to revisit the core concepts of API development. An API acts as an intermediary between different software applications, facilitating seamless communication and data exchange. There are various types of APIs, including RESTful APIs, GraphQL, SOAP, and WebSockets, each serving unique purposes.

9.1.1 Evolution of APIs

The evolution of APIs has been driven by the need for scalability, interoperability, and efficient data management. With the rise of microservices architecture and cloud computing, APIs are now central to application design. Understanding how APIs have evolved and their role within modern application architectures is crucial for developing robust solutions.

9.2 Designing APIs for Scalability

A well-designed API is not only functional but also scalable. Scalability ensures that the API can handle increased loads without compromising performance. Key considerations include:

9.2.1 Versioning

API versioning is critical when introducing new features or making breaking changes. By maintaining multiple versions of an API, developers can provide backward compatibility, allowing legacy clients to continue functioning seamlessly.

9.2.2 Rate Limiting

To prevent abuse and ensure fair usage, implementing rate limiting is essential. This technique restricts the number of requests a user can make in a given timeframe, helping to protect the API from potential overload and ensuring equitable access for all users.

9.2.3 Caching

Caching responses can dramatically improve API performance. By storing frequently accessed data temporarily, APIs can reduce latency and minimize backend load. Techniques such as HTTP caching, content delivery networks (CDNs), and application-level caching (e.g., Redis) ought to be employed strategically.

9.3 Security Best Practices

Security is paramount in API development. APIs are often targeted by attackers seeking unauthorized access to sensitive data. To mitigate risks, consider the following practices:

9.3.1 Authentication and Authorization

Implement robust authentication (identifying users) and authorization (granting permissions) mechanisms. Popular methods include OAuth 2.0, JWT (JSON Web Tokens), and API keys. Choose an approach that aligns with project requirements while ensuring the least privilege principle.

9.3.2 Data Encryption

Data transmitted via APIs should be encrypted, both in transit and at rest. Utilize protocols like HTTPS for secure data transmission and encrypt sensitive information stored in databases.

9.3.3 Input Validation and Sanitization

Always validate and sanitize input data to protect against common vulnerabilities, such as SQL injection and cross-site scripting (XSS). Employ frameworks and libraries that provide built-in security features to strengthen your API.

9.4 Documentation and Developer Experience

Comprehensive API documentation is essential for a successful API. Developers rely on clear and concise documentation to understand endpoints, data structures, and usage examples. Employ tools such as Swagger/OpenAPI or Postman for creating interactive API documentation.

9.4.1 Developer Portals

Consider creating a developer portal where consumers can access documentation, monitor usage stats, and even try out endpoints in a sandbox environment. A well-designed portal enhances the developer experience and fosters easier adoption of the API.

9.5 Testing and Monitoring

Ensuring the reliability of your API requires rigorous testing and monitoring. Incorporate testing into the development lifecycle using automated tests to validate functionality and performance.

9.5.1 Automated Testing

Unit tests and integration tests should be an integral part of your workflow. Utilize frameworks like JUnit, Mocha, or pytest, depending on your programming language of choice, to automate testing processes.

9.5.2 Monitoring and Analytics

Real-time monitoring tools allow developers to track API performance, error rates, and usage patterns. Implement analytics to gain insights on user interactions and identify areas for improvement.

9.6 Utilizing Modern Tools and Frameworks

The world of API development is rich with frameworks and tools designed to streamline the development process. Technologies like Express.js for Node.js, Django REST Framework for Python, and Spring Boot for Java provide robust solutions for building APIs quickly and efficiently.

9.6.1 Serverless Architecture

Further enhancing the potential of APIs, serverless architecture allows developers to focus on writing code without managing the underlying infrastructure. Platforms like AWS Lambda, Google Cloud Functions, and Azure Functions simplify deployment and scalability.

As we conclude this chapter on advanced API development for backend development, it's clear that creating a robust and scalable API requires a blend of strategic design, security considerations, and ongoing monitoring. By understanding the evolving landscape of APIs and employing best practices, developers can build APIs that not only meet current needs but also adapt to future challenges.

Designing RESTful APIs with Groovy

In the modern era of web development, creating efficient and scalable APIs is crucial for facilitating communication between different services. REST (Representational State Transfer) has emerged as a popular architectural style because of its simplicity and alignment with the stateless nature of the web. Groovy, a dynamic language for the Java platform, provides powerful features that make the design and implementation of RESTful APIs straightforward and enjoyable.

This chapter will guide you through the process of architecting RESTful APIs using Groovy, focusing on best practices, essential features of the language, and practical examples.

Understanding RESTful APIs

Before jumping into Groovy, let's clarify what RESTful APIs are. A RESTful API adheres to the following principles:

Statelessness: Each request from a client to the server must contain all the information needed to understand and process it. Sessions will not be stored on the server.

Resource-Based: Everything in REST is treated as a resource, which can be represented by a unique URI (Uniform Resource Identifier). Resources can be data entitics such as users, products, or articles.

Use of Standard HTTP Methods: RESTful APIs use standard HTTP methods to manipulate resources:

GET: Retrieve a resource.

POST: Create a new resource.

PUT: Update an existing resource.

DELETE: Remove a resource.

Representation: Resources can be represented in various formats, such as JSON or XML, but JSON is the most commonly used due to its lightweight structure and ease of use with JavaScript.

Setting Up Your Groovy Environment

To get started with Groovy for backend development, you need to set up your environment. Follow the steps below:

Install Groovy: Download and install Groovy from the official [Groovy website](http://groovy-lang.org/download.html). Ensure that it is added to your system's PATH.

Choose a Framework: While Groovy can be used standalone, using a framework can significantly speed up the development process. Some popular frameworks for building RESTful APIs in Groovy include:

Grails: A web application framework that leverages Groovy and is built on top of the Spring framework.

Ratpack: A lightweight framework designed for fast, scalable web applications and services.

Set Up a Project: If you are using Grails, create a new project using the command:

```groovy
grails create-app my-rest-api
```

146

```
```

For a Ratpack application, create a new project using:

```groovy
gradle init --type basic
```

Creating Your First RESTful API ### Step 1: Define Your Resources

For our example, let's create a simple API for managing a list of books. Each book will have an ID, a title, and an author.

Step 2: Implementing the Model

In your Groovy application, you can define a Book class:

```groovy class Book {
Long id String title String author
}
```

Step 3: Creating the Controller

In a Grails application, you would create a controller like this:

```groovy
class BookController {
def books = [] // Simulating a database
def index() {
```

```
render books as JSON
}
def show(Long id) {
def book = books.find { it.id == id } if (book) {
render book as JSON
} else {
render status: 404
}
}
def save() {
def book = new Book(params) books << book
render book as JSON, status: 201
}
def update(Long id) {
def book = books.find { it.id == id } if (book) {
book.properties = params

render book as JSON
} else {
render status: 404
}
}
def delete(Long id) {
```

```groovy
def book = books.find { it.id == id } if (book) {
books.remove(book) render status: 204
} else {
render status: 404
}
}
}
```
```

In a Ratpack application, your route definitions might look like this:
```groovy
import ratpack.groovy.Groovy.ratpack
ratpack {
def books = []
handlers { get("books") {
respond books
}
get("books/:id") {
def book = books.find { it.id == path.id.toLong() } if (book) {
respond book
} else {
render status: 404
}
```

149
```

```
}
post("books") {
books << parse(Book) render status: 201
}
put("books/:id") {
def book = books.find { it.id == path.id.toLong() } if
(book) {
book.properties = parse(Book) respond book
} else {
render status: 404
}


}
delete("books/:id") {
def book = books.find { it.id == path.id.toLong() } if
(book) {
books.remove(book) render status: 204
} else {
render status: 404
}
}
}
}
```
```
```

In these examples, the API provides endpoints to create, read, update, and delete books, adhering to the RESTful principles.

Step 4: Testing Your API

You can use tools like Postman or cURL to test your API endpoints.

To retrieve all books: Send a GET request to `http://localhost:8080/books`

To add a new book: Send a POST request with JSON body to `http://localhost:8080/books`

To update a book: Send a PUT request with the updated JSON to `http://localhost:8080/books/{id}`

To delete a book: Send a DELETE request to `http://localhost:8080/books/{id}` ## Error Handling and Validation

In real applications, it's essential to implement error handling and validation. For instance, checking if the incoming request contains valid data before processing it. Use Groovy's built-in features for validation:

```groovy
def save() {

if (!params.title || !params.author) {

render status: 400, text: "Title and Author are required."
return

}


// Proceed to save

}
```

```
```

This chapter has provided you with the fundamentals of building a simple RESTful API, including setting up your environment, defining resources, and handling standard operations in an API. As you advance, consider exploring more complex use cases, such as authentication, pagination, and data serialization, to build fully functional APIs capable of handling real-world applications. Enjoy leveraging Groovy's features and the simplicity of RESTful design in your backend development journey!

Adding GraphQL Support for Flexible APIs

Traditional REST APIs, while effective, often struggle with scalability and can lead to over-fetching or under-fetching of data. GraphQL offers a compelling alternative by allowing clients to request exactly the data they need, enabling more dynamic and efficient communication between front-end and back-end systems.

This chapter focuses on adding GraphQL support to a Groovy-based backend, leveraging the strengths of Groovy along with existing libraries and frameworks that facilitate the implementation of GraphQL in a seamless manner. We will walk through the essentials of setting up a GraphQL server in Groovy, define our schema, and handle queries and mutations, all while maintaining the simplicity and readability characteristic of Groovy.

1. Understanding GraphQL

Before diving into implementation, let's conceptualize

GraphQL. Originally developed by Facebook in 2012 and released as an open-source project in 2015, GraphQL is a query language for APIs as well as a server- side runtime for executing those queries. The key features that make GraphQL attractive include:

Single Endpoint: Unlike REST APIs that typically expose multiple endpoints, GraphQL operates through a single endpoint, which simplifies API management.

Flexible Queries: Clients can structure their requests to specify exactly which data they need, avoiding excessive or insufficient data transfers.

Strong Typing: GraphQL is strongly typed, and its schema can be introspected. This allows developers to understand the data structure available to them.

2. Setting Up the Groovy Environment

To build our backend with GraphQL support in Groovy, we need to set up a suitable environment. The common toolchain includes:

Groovy Language: Ensure you have Groovy installed on your system. You can run Groovy scripts using SDKMAN! or the Groovy distribution from its official site.

Spring Boot: We'll use Spring Boot to manage the application lifecycle and simplify dependency management. Create a new Spring Boot application using Spring Initializer or set it up manually.

GraphQL Dependencies: Add the necessary GraphQL dependencies to your `build.gradle` file:

```groovy dependencies {
```

```
implementation 'org.springframework.boot:spring-boot-
starter-web'      implementation      'com.graphql-java-
kickstart:graphql-spring-boot-starter:12.0.0'
implementation 'org.springframework.boot:spring-boot-
starter'

}
```
```

## 3. Defining the Schema

GraphQL operates on a schema that defines the types of
data you can query and the relationships between those
types. Our next step is to define a schema for our
application.

Create a file called `schema.graphqls` in the
`src/main/resources/graphql` directory. Here's a simple
example schema for a blog application:

```graphql type Post { id: ID!
```

title: String! content: String! author: Author!

}

type Author { id: ID!

name: String! posts: [Post!]!

}

type Query { allPosts: [Post!]! post(id: ID!): Post

}

type Mutation {

createPost(title: String!, content: String!, authorId: ID!):
```

Post!

}

```

### Explanation of the Schema

**Types**: The `Post` and `Author` types represent the core entities in our blog application.

**Queries**: The `Query` type allows us to fetch all posts or a single post by its ID.

**Mutations**: The `Mutation` type defines how to create new posts. ## 4. Implementing Resolvers

Resolvers are functions that provide the logic for fetching the data as specified by the GraphQL queries. Create a new Groovy class called `PostResolver.groovy` that implements the necessary resolvers.

```groovy
import graphql.kickstart.annotations.GraphQLApi import org.springframework.stereotype.Component

@GraphQLApi @Component
class PostResolver {
private final PostService postService


PostResolver(PostService postService) { this.postService = postService
}
List<Post> allPosts() {
return postService.findAll()
```
```

```groovy
}
Post post(Long id) {

return postService.findById(id)

}
Post createPost(String title, String content, Long authorId) {

return postService.save(new Post(title: title, content: content, authorId: authorId))

}
}
```

Explanation of Resolvers

The `PostResolver` class connects our schema with data through `postService`, which contains the actual data-fetching logic.

5. Creating the Service Layer

To separate concerns, create a service layer that encapsulates the business logic. The `PostService` can be implemented as follows:

```groovy
import org.springframework.stereotype.Service

@Service

class PostService {

private final List<Post> posts = [] private Long currentId = 1
```

```
List<Post> findAll() { return posts
}
Post findById(Long id) {
return posts.find { it.id == id }
}
Post save(Post post) { post.id = currentId++ posts << post
return post
}
}
```
```

## 6. Testing the GraphQL API

Now that we've implemented our GraphQL support, we'll want to test it. Spring Boot, along with GraphQL Java Tools, provides an easy way to do this. You can use tools like Postman or Insomnia to construct queries against your GraphQL endpoint.

For instance, a query to fetch all posts would look like this:

```graphql query {
allPosts { id
title content author {
name
}
}
```
```

```
}
```
` ` `

And a mutation to create a new post could be executed like:

```graphql mutation {
```

createPost(title: "New Title", content: "Content goes here", authorId: "1") { id

title

```
}
```

```
}
```
` ` `

In this chapter, we've explored the integration of GraphQL into a Groovy backend. By defining a schema, creating resolvers and services, and testing our GraphQL API, we have leveraged Groovy's simplicity and effectiveness to build flexible APIs that cater to dynamic client requests.

Chapter 10: Error Handling and Debugging

The ability to efficiently identify, diagnose, and resolve issues can significantly impact the performance and reliability of your applications. In this chapter, we will delve into the strategies and best practices for managing errors and debugging your Groovy applications, making you more adept at building robust backend systems.

11.1 Understanding Errors and Exceptions

Errors and exceptions are conditions that disrupt the normal flow of your application. In Groovy, as in many other languages, it is crucial to differentiate between the two:

Errors: These are serious issues that are typically beyond the control of the application, such as system-level failures. They signal problems that are not intended to be caught or handled by the application.

Exceptions: These are conditions that a program might want to catch and handle. They usually occur due to programmatic errors, invalid input, or other unforeseen circumstances that can be anticipated.

11.1.1 Types of Exceptions in Groovy

Groovy follows the Java exception hierarchy, thus it has checked exceptions (which need to be declared) and unchecked exceptions (which do not). Understanding the types of exceptions will help in devising adequate handling mechanisms:

Checked Exceptions: These are exceptions that must be either caught or declared in the method signature. Examples include `IOException` and `SQLException`.

Unchecked Exceptions: These are exceptions that do not require explicit handling, like

`NullPointerException` or `ArrayIndexOutOfBoundsException`. They are often caused by bugs and should be resolved in the code rather than caught.

11.2 Structured Error Handling with Try-Catch Blocks

In Groovy, the primary mechanism for handling exceptions is the `try-catch` block. It allows developers to encapsulate code that may throw exceptions and define how to deal with these exceptions.

```groovy
try {
// Code that may throw an exception def result = riskyOperation()
} catch (SpecificException ex) {
// Handle specific exception
log.error("A specific error occurred: ${ex.message}", ex)
} catch (Exception ex) {
// Handle general exceptions
log.error("An error occurred: ${ex.message}", ex)
} finally {
// Code that will always execute, regardless of success or
```

failure cleanupResources()

}
```

### 11.2.1 Using `finally`

The `finally` block is especially useful for releasing resources such as database connections or file handles. It guarantees execution regardless of whether an exception is thrown, which is fundamental for maintaining system stability.

## 11.3 Groovy's Built-in Exception Handling Features

Groovy provides several enhancements over Java in the realm of exception handling. These include: ### 11.3.1 `@SuppressWarnings`

To suppress specific compiler warnings regarding exceptions, you can use the `@SuppressWarnings` annotation. This is particularly useful when you deliberately ignore certain exceptions, although it should be used judiciously.

### 11.3.2 The `throw` and `throws` Keywords

The `throw` keyword is used to explicitly throw an exception, which is vital for custom exception handling in your application logic:

```groovy
if (!validInput(input)) {

throw new IllegalArgumentException("Invalid Input Provided")

}
```
```

```
```

The `throws` keyword can be used in method signatures to indicate that a method might throw exceptions:

```groovy
void riskyMethod() throws IOException {

// method implementation

}
```

11.4 Logging Exceptions

Logging is essential for understanding application behavior in production. Groovy facilitates easy logging through frameworks like Log4j or SLF4J. Here is a basic example of using SLF4J for logging exceptions:

```groovy
import org.slf4j.Logger

import org.slf4j.LoggerFactory

class MyService {

private static final Logger log = LoggerFactory.getLogger(MyService)

void execute() { try {

// logic that might throw an exception

} catch (Exception e) {

log.error("Error during execution: {}", e.getMessage(), e)

}
```

```
}
}
```
` ` `

11.5 Debugging Techniques

Debugging is essential to troubleshoot and fix issues effectively. Groovy offers several powerful tools and techniques for debugging applications.

11.5.1 Using Integrated Development Environments (IDEs)

IDEs like IntelliJ IDEA or Eclipse provide robust debugging tools, allowing developers to set breakpoints, inspect variables, and step through code execution. Familiarity with these tools can enhance your debugging prowess significantly.

11.5.2 Utilizing the Groovy Console

The Groovy Console is a powerful tool for testing snippets of Groovy code. It allows you to execute code interactively, helping to identify issues in isolated blocks without deploying the entire application.

11.5.3 Assertions

Using assertions can help catch errors by validating assumptions in your code. In Groovy, assertions can be utilized straightforwardly:

```groovy
assert myCondition : "Condition failed"
```

Assertions should be used during development and can be

163

disabled in production for performance considerations.

11.6 Custom Exception Handling

Creating custom exceptions can provide more context regarding errors specific to your application's domain. By extending the `Exception` class, you can create tailored exception types:

```groovy
class MyCustomException extends Exception {
MyCustomException(String message) {
super(message)
}
}
```

Utilizing custom exceptions can enhance your error monitoring and allow you to create distinct handling paths based on specific error conditions.

11.7 Best Practices for Error Handling and Debugging

Log Exceptions: Always log exceptions with sufficient detail to facilitate investigation.

Use Specific Exception Types: Catch specific exceptions rather than broad ones to avoid masking other potential issues.

Fail Fast: Anticipate and handle potential errors early in processing to prevent cascading failures.

Write Tests: Use unit and integration tests to validate expectancies and ensure errors are caught proactively.

Review and Refactor: Regularly review error handling and logging practices as part of code reviews to incorporate lessons learned from past errors.

By mastering the techniques outlined in this chapter, from structured exception handling to utilizing the advantages of a debugging IDE, you can create more resilient applications. Understanding how exceptions work, logging information purposefully, and employing best practices will not only streamline your development process but also enhance the overall user experience.

Best Practices for Handling Exceptions in Groovy

This chapter will cover the best practices for handling exceptions in Groovy, focusing on how to write robust, maintainable, and user-friendly backend applications.

Understanding Exceptions

Before diving into best practices, it's essential to understand what exceptions are and how they function in Groovy. Exceptions are events that occur during the execution of a program that disrupts its normal flow. In Groovy, exceptions can be caught and handled using try-catch blocks, similar to Java, but with Groovy's unique features that add flexibility and simplicity.

Types of Exceptions

Checked Exceptions: These exceptions are checked at compile-time. Examples include

`IOException` and `SQLException`. They must be declared in the method signature if they are thrown.

Unchecked Exceptions: These exceptions are not checked at compile-time. Examples include

`NullPointerException` and `ArrayIndexOutOfBoundsException`. They typically indicate programming errors.

Runtime Exceptions: A subclass of unchecked exceptions that can occur during the application's runtime. These can often be avoided with proper coding practices.

Best Practices for Handling Exceptions ### 1. Use Specific Exceptions

Instead of catching generic exceptions, aim to catch specific types. This can help in identifying the root cause of issues quickly and allows for more granular handling.

```groovy
try {
// Code that may throw an exception
} catch (FileNotFoundException e) {
// Handle file not found specifically
} catch (IOException e) {
// Handle other IO issues
} catch (Exception e) {
// Handle all other exceptions
}
```

2. Avoid Catching Exception Too Broadly

Catching `Exception` or `Throwable` broadly can mask

issues in your code. It is important to understand that this practice hides the specific problem that occurred, making debugging more difficult.

3. Use Custom Exceptions

For scenarios specific to your application, create custom exception classes that extend `Exception` or

`RuntimeException`. This makes it easier to differentiate between types of failures.

```groovy
class UserNotFoundException extends RuntimeException
{ UserNotFoundException(String message) {

super(message)

}
}
```

4. Logging Exceptions

Log the exceptions you catch. This practice is essential for debugging and monitoring. Use a logging framework, such as SLF4J combined with Logback or Log4J, to capture stack traces and error messages.

```groovy
import org.slf4j.Logger

import org.slf4j.LoggerFactory

class UserService {

private    static    final    Logger    logger    =
```
167

```
LoggerFactory.getLogger(UserService)

void findUser(String userId) { try {

// Code that may throw an exception

} catch (UserNotFoundException e) { logger.error("User
not found: {}", userId, e) throw e // rethrow if necessary

}

}

}
```
` ` `

5. Clean Up Resources

When handling exceptions, you may need to release
resources like database connections or file handlers.
Groovy provides a convenient way to do this via the
`withResource` construct or the try-with-resources
pattern in Java, ensuring that resources are closed
properly.

` ` `groovy
```
File file = new File("data.txt") file.withReader { reader ->

// Read data

}
```
` ` `

6. Fail Fast and Provide Feedback

Instead of allowing a system to run in an error state, favor
a fail-fast approach. Detect issues early, provide
meaningful feedback to users, and, where applicable,
return informative messages through the API.

7. Centralized Exception Handling

Consider implementing a centralized exception handling approach, such as using Filters or Interceptors in web applications. This approach makes maintaining the error handling code simpler and reduces redundancy.

```groovy
class GlobalExceptionHandler {
def handleException(Exception e) {
// Centralized error handling logic
}
}
```

8. Use the Groovy's `@Grab` for Dependency Management

By utilizing Groovy's `@Grab` annotation for dependency management, you can manage exceptions thrown due to missing dependencies more effectively.

```groovy
@Grab('org.slf4j:slf4j-api:1.7.30')
```

9. Validate Inputs Early

Validation should be performed at the entry points of your application to ensure that exceptions are less likely to occur downstream. This can involve checking parameters for nulls, ensuring types match expectations, etc.

10. Write Unit Tests for Exception Handling

Writing unit tests will help ensure that your exception-handling logic works as intended. Test various scenarios, including success cases, expected failures, and edge cases.

```groovy
class UserServiceTest {

UserService userService = new UserService()

void "should throw UserNotFoundException when user not found"() { when:

userService.findUser("non-existent-id")

then: thrown(UserNotFoundException)

}

}
```

Effective exception handling in Groovy is vital for developing resilient backend applications. By following these best practices, including using specific exceptions, logging, and centralized handling, developers can create applications that are not only more robust but easier to maintain and debug. These practices will help ensure that your backend services deliver reliable functionality even when faced with unexpected issues.

With Groovy's flexibility and dynamic nature, you can implement these strategies consistently to build a strong foundation for your applications.

Debugging Tips for Efficient Problem Solving

Debugging is an essential part of the software development lifecycle. In backend development, a well-performing application relies on the seamless integration of multiple components, and understanding how to debug effectively can save both time and frustration. Groovy, a dynamic language for the Java platform, offers unique features that can enhance debugging processes. This chapter will cover essential debugging tips tailored for Groovy, focusing on how to diagnose issues swiftly and efficiently in backend development.

Understanding the Basics of Debugging in Groovy

Before diving into debugging techniques, it is important to understand the nature of the issues you might encounter in Groovy applications. Common problems include:

Syntax errors

Null pointer exceptions

Logic errors

Integration issues with databases, web services, or other APIs ### Utilizing IDE Debugging Tools

Most Integrated Development Environments (IDEs) support Groovy and provide robust debugging tools. Popular IDEs like IntelliJ IDEA and Eclipse offer features such as breakpoints, watch expressions, and step-through debugging.

Setting Breakpoints

A breakpoint allows you to pause execution at a specific

line of code. This is particularly useful for examining state and flow before reaching a problematic area:

Set breakpoints on lines of code where you suspect issues may arise.

Run your application in debug mode to halt execution at these breakpoints.

Inspect variable values, call stacks, and evaluate expressions in real-time. #### Step Through Your Code

Use "Step Into", "Step Over", and "Step Out" functionalities to control the flow of execution. This allows you to examine how various parts of your code interact and to locate the source of issues.

Leverage Groovy's Dynamic Nature

Groovy's dynamic features can make debugging easier, but they can also introduce complexity. Consider the following strategies to leverage its strengths:

Use Closures for Scoping: Closures in Groovy can help localize variables and reduce side effects. This clarity simplifies debugging by controlling where and how variables are accessed.


```groovy
def processData(List data) { data.each { item ->
println "Processing: ${item}"
// Additional logic here
```

```
}
}
```

Type Checking in Groovy: While Groovy allows dynamic typing, explicit type definitions can aid debugging. Using `@TypeChecked` can help catch type-related issues at compile time rather than runtime.

Dynamic Method Dispatching: Be cautious with dynamic method dispatching. If you are overloading methods, ensure the signatures are clear to avoid unexpected method resolutions, leading to confusing runtime errors.

Implement Logging Strategically

Effective logging can be a lifeline for debugging. Groovy supports various logging frameworks that can be easily integrated, such as SLF4J and Log4j.

Log at Different Levels: Use different levels of logging (e.g., INFO, DEBUG, WARN, ERROR) appropriately to categorize messages for better clarity.

```groovy
log.debug("Debugging process started") log.info("User data received: ${userData}")
```

Conditional Logging: Implement conditional logging to avoid cluttering log files. This can be achieved using additional flags or properties to toggle output.

Structured Logging: Format your logs to include timestamps, log levels, and contextual information. This practice helps in diagnosing issues when reviewing logs later.

Testing and Assertion Practices

Testing your code thoroughly can significantly reduce the number of bugs in your application. Groovy's built-in testing features, especially with frameworks like Spock, facilitate this process.

Unit Testing with Spock: Write comprehensive unit tests for your methods to catch errors early. Spock's expressive syntax makes defining expectations straightforward.

```groovy
class UserServiceSpec extends Specification { def userService = new UserService()

def "test user retrieval"() { expect:

userService.getUser(1) == expectedUser

}

}
```

Use Assertions: In scenarios where tests are not feasible, use assertions to validate assumptions dynamically. This practice can help catch logical errors.

```groovy
assert user != null : "User object is null"


```

Profiling and Performance Monitoring

Sometimes, bugs manifest as performance issues. Using profiling tools specific to Groovy or JVM monitoring can help identify bottlenecks.

- Tools like VisualVM can give insight into memory usage, thread activity, and CPU usage. Profiling your application can lead to uncovering hidden bugs that only surface under load.

Community and Resources

Leverage community resources for additional support. Groovy has a vibrant community with plenty of forums, GitHub projects, and documentation available. When stuck, seeking help from others can provide new perspectives on the issue.

By implementing the tips discussed in this chapter—effective use of IDE tools, understanding Groovy's dynamic nature, strategic logging, thorough testing, and profiling—developers can enhance their debugging efficiency. Embracing these strategies will not only aid in immediate problem resolution but also contribute to a more robust overall development process, leading to cleaner and more maintainable code.

Conclusion

As we conclude this journey through the Groovy programming language and its applications in backend development, it's clear that Groovy stands out as a powerful tool that enables developers to create robust and efficient applications. Throughout this book, we have explored the many facets of Groovy—from its concise syntax and dynamic typing to its seamless integration with existing Java code and the rich ecosystem that surrounds it.

We've delved into the ways Groovy can simplify complex tasks, enhance productivity, and foster a clean, maintainable codebase. Whether you are building RESTful APIs, microservices, or leveraging frameworks like Grails, Groovy proves to be an invaluable asset in any backend developer's toolkit. Its expressive nature not only makes writing code quicker and easier but also allows for greater creativity in problem-solving.

Moreover, the possibility to harness Groovy's capabilities through testing frameworks and tools opens doors to robust development practices, emphasizing the importance of code quality and reliability. With Groovy's unique features, such as closures, language extensions, and powerful DSL capabilities, developers are empowered to craft solutions that are not only effective but also elegantly designed.

As you move forward in your programming journey, we encourage you to actively experiment with Groovy, delve deeper into its community, and embrace the innovations it brings to the sphere of backend development. The landscape of technology is ever-evolving, and Groovy is poised to play an instrumental role in shaping the future of backend solutions.

In summary, Groovy is not just a programming language; it's a paradigm shift that can revolutionize the way you approach backend development. By embracing Groovy, you're not merely learning a new language—you're adopting a new philosophy of programming that prioritizes simplicity, efficiency, and creativity. May your Groovy journey lead you to new heights in your development career, and may your applications shine with the brilliance that Groovy has to offer. Happy coding!

Biography

Davis Simon is a passionate software developer, seasoned backend architect, and advocate for clean, efficient code. With over a decade of experience in web application development, Davis has built scalable, high-performing systems for startups and enterprises alike. His expertise lies in backend development and leveraging the power of languages like Groovy to create APIs and microservices that are as robust as they are elegant.

A self-proclaimed "Groovy enthusiast," Davis discovered the language early in his career and quickly fell in love with its versatility and simplicity. His dedication to Groovy programming inspired him to write this book and share his insights with aspiring developers looking to harness its potential for backend development.

When he's not writing code or crafting the next big web application, Davis enjoys exploring emerging technologies, mentoring new developers, and experimenting with creative ways to solve programming challenges. Outside of the tech world, Davis is an avid gamer and a lover of all things sci-fi, often finding inspiration for his projects in futuristic tales and virtual worlds.

With this eBook, Davis invites you to join him on a

journey to revolutionize backend development with Groovy. His approachable teaching style and practical advice will empower you to take your skills to the next level—whether you're building your first API or architecting complex systems.

Glossary: Groovy for Backend Development

1. Groovy

Groovy is an agile and dynamic language for the Java Virtual Machine (JVM) that enhances the Java platform's capabilities. It features a syntax that is easy to learn and write, making it a popular choice among Java developers and those looking for a more concise way to implement backend solutions.

2. Syntax Sugar

Syntax sugar refers to syntax within a programming language that is designed to make things easier to read or express. Groovy incorporates syntax sugar that simplifies common programming constructs, reducing boilerplate code and making for cleaner, more readable programs.

3. Closure

A closure in Groovy is a block of code that can be assigned to a variable and executed at a later point. Closures can take parameters, modify variables, and return values. They are essential for creating concise syntax in Groovy, particularly when dealing with functional programming paradigms.

4. GORM (Grails Object-Relational Mapping)

GORM is a part of the Grails framework that provides a powerful and easy-to-use object-relational mapping capability for Groovy applications. It allows developers to interact with databases using Groovy domain classes, eliminating the need for extensive SQL queries.

5. DSL (Domain Specific Language)

A Domain Specific Language is a programming language specialized to a particular application domain. Groovy's flexibility allows developers to create their own DSLs, which can simplify complex tasks by providing a more intuitive and focused syntax for specific use cases.

6. Dynamic Typing

Dynamic typing is a feature of Groovy that allows variable types to be determined at runtime rather than at compile time. This flexibility can lead to faster coding and prototyping but may introduce errors that would be caught in statically typed languages like Java.

7. Groovy Scripts

Groovy scripts are files containing Groovy code that can be executed without the need for compilation. This feature makes Groovy an excellent choice for scripting tasks, rapid prototyping, and automation within backend systems.

8. Gradle

Gradle is a build automation tool that is often used in conjunction with Groovy, particularly in Java and JVM-based projects. It allows developers to manage

179

dependencies, compile code, run tests, and package applications efficiently. Groovy's DSL capabilities can create custom build scripts in a readable format.

9. Spring Framework

The Spring Framework is a popular Java-based framework that provides comprehensive infrastructure support for developing Java applications. Groovy can be seamlessly integrated with Spring, allowing developers to write Spring components in a more concise and expressive manner.

10. Spock

Spock is a testing framework for Java and Groovy applications that provides a specification and testing style different from traditional JUnit tests. It integrates easily with Groovy and allows for writing clean, readable test cases to verify the functionality of backend services.

11. Markup Builder

The Markup Builder is a Groovy class that simplifies the creation of XML and HTML content. It provides a convenient syntax that allows developers to generate well-structured markup in a programmatic way, which is particularly useful for web services and APIs.

12. Groovy EE (Enterprise Edition)

Groovy EE refers to the use of Groovy within the context of enterprise applications, often in conjunction with Java EE technologies. This combination leverages Groovy's strengths while retaining the robustness and scalability of Java EE, facilitating the development of large-scale backend systems.

13. AST (Abstract Syntax Tree)

An Abstract Syntax Tree is a data structure that represents the structure of code in a hierarchical form. Groovy utilizes AST transformations to provide features like annotations and compile-time metaprogramming, enhancing its capabilities without sacrificing performance.

14. Metaprogramming

Metaprogramming is the practice of writing code that can modify its own structure or behavior at runtime. Groovy's metaprogramming capabilities allow developers to create dynamic behaviors, customize class definitions, and extend existing classes without altering the original code.

15. Grails

Grails is a web application framework based on Groovy and designed for building modern web applications with a focus on developer productivity. It integrates seamlessly with the Spring framework and follows convention over configuration principles, allowing developers to get projects up and running quickly.

www.ingramcontent.com/pod-product-compliance
Lightning Source LLC
Chambersburg PA
CBHW070948050326
40689CB00014B/3393